BECOME A BETTER WRITER

How to write with clarity and simplicity

Donald Powers & Greg Rosenberg

Published in South Africa
by Clarity Global Strategic Communications (Pty) Ltd

Distributed by Cover2Cover Books
www.cover2cover.co.za

Print ISBN: 978-1-928466-16-1
E-book ISBN: 978-1-928466-17-8

Cover design by Georgia Demertzis
Typesetting and layout by Firebrand
Cover images © Shutterstock

Clarity Global Strategic Communications (Pty) Ltd
Company registration no. 2019/175661/07
Unit 1, Demar Square, 45 Bell Crescent,
Westlake Business Park, Westlake, Cape Town, 7945
+27 21 702 11 77
www.clarityglobal.net

CONTENTS

FOREWORD

By Redi Tlhabi

Words matter. They have consequences. They can make or break our hopes. They can polarise and cause irreparable harm. But words can also inspire us and open up a whole new world. We can travel to different destinations, sample cultures and respond to humanity's most urgent needs through words and writing.

If we want readers and audiences to choose us again and again, then this is a good book to read. Donald Powers and Greg Rosenberg remind us that knowing how to choose and use the right words can have consequences far beyond what we may imagine.

Anyone who has ever written a book, report, presentation, article or even a speech has probably spent a considerable amount of time staring at the blank computer screen thinking, "I know what I want to say, but how do I say it?!" In today's world, technological advances mean writers are competing with various forms of content, produced in a short space of time, across multiple platforms. Our potential readers are spoilt for choice when it comes to accessing content and reading material. We are even competing with content where a story can be told with images, video and graphics rather than words. The pressure on writers to adapt and sharpen their skills has never been greater.

We are not entitled to our readers' indulgence. *Become a Better Writer* gives us the tools to help us improve our craft and turn stories, information and experiences into gripping tales or meaningful reports. If you have been stuck with a great message or a powerful story that you could not translate into accessible language, then this book is for you.

This is a unique little volume. It is not your typical "how to" manual. First, the authors have a delightful sense of humour. Second, they are great at following their own advice: "Don't test your reader's patience" – be concise and get to the point. The third feature is particularly relevant for me – I always have too much to say and too little time and space in which to say it. So how does a writer and public speaker like myself know what to prioritise and what to leave out? The authors deftly answer this conundrum with clear and practical tips on how to choose only the most relevant and impactful content when writing.

One attribute that distinguishes this book from others is the authors' convincing linking of clear messaging to socio-political and economic outcomes. How can citizens participate in political processes unless they understand the decisions that are made on their behalf? Powers and Rosenberg remind us that lucid and accessible writing can be a matter of life and death in regions where democracy and accountability are fragile. When humanity's actions threaten our planet, writing a persuasive message can lead to enduring behavioural change.

This is a book for all types of writers – and all types of writing. If you are in the public or development sector and wonder why public discourse does not reflect your policies, then this book is a must-read! If you are a novelist or non-fiction writer who has watched helplessly as mundane stories gain far more traction than your work, then *Become a Better Writer* can help you achieve that much-needed breakthrough. Academics will also learn some valuable lessons on how to write for the reader and make their highly cerebral content concise, informative and engaging. As an experienced writer, I was particularly excited and challenged by the chapter on using narrative and varying your style.

A writer never quite "arrives". Our relationship with words is an ongoing journey, which can become stale and predictable too. This book has given me fresh eyes and renewed energy to perfect my craft – it has been worth every minute!

INTRODUCTION

About you

You can write better. We all can. Improving the quality of your writing starts with rethinking your assumptions and developing healthier writing habits. This book will help you do both.

The three most common problems in non-fiction writing are using too many words, being unnecessarily complicated and not thinking about who you are writing for.

Much writing is tediously long-winded. All of us have been on the receiving end of this practice, but few of us have the time or patience to endure it. Don't waste your reader's time. This book will help you to write more concisely.

We all know what it's like when you ask a doctor, a mechanic or an information technology specialist to explain something but their answer only adds to your confusion. The problem is not what they know but *how* they communicate *what* they know to you, the non-specialist. It's often assumed that using big words and long sentences will impress your reader. That's a mistake. Albert Einstein is sometimes credited with having said that if you can't explain something simply, you don't understand it well enough. Challenging yourself to write as clearly as possible will help you to think more clearly.

Non-fiction writing is rarely an exercise in self-expression. Chances are that you're not writing for yourself: you're writing for your readers. Understanding who you're writing for is just as important as knowing what you want to say.

Writing simply and clearly is not easy: it takes patience, practice and care. The purpose of this book is to support you. It contains principles, examples, anecdotes and tips that you can adopt to improve your writing craft.

About us

At Clarity Global Strategic Communications, we help our clients communicate with clarity, simplicity and integrity. That's not a marketing slogan: it's a way to make a real impact that supports democracy, transparency and accountability in every field of human endeavour.

Whether we're working on an editing or writing project, our goal is to produce a text that is crisp, clear and engaging. Sometimes material we receive for editing requires a light touch; at other times it requires major surgery. In each case, we have to keep in mind the client's intended message and their target audience. We know how much time, thinking and rewriting can go into making a good sentence. We've also learnt many lessons the hard way – through experience. We'd like to share some of these lessons with you.

About this book

You'll find a great many books on writing – though few of them are great. This one is designed as a practical tool for those who wish to improve their craft. The authors have extensive experience as writers and editors. Our focus is on non-fiction writing, though the book will also be useful to writers of fiction.

You can read this book from front to back, or you can skip between sections with abandon. A handy index is available for quick reference. The examples we discuss are derived from real-world material and are particularly relevant to the African context. Many of the examples we use are based on client material we have edited. Don't worry if you have little knowledge of a particular field: our discussion of each example will highlight issues that are relevant to all types of writing. We've drawn the examples from different kinds of writing (including reports, essays, emails, novels and speeches) across a wide range of subjects.

Here's an overview of the book's contents:

- **CHAPTER 1** outlines the common problems that nearly all writers encounter at some stage. We discuss the problem of writing to impress rather than inform, consider the global trend towards using plain language, and highlight some features of good and bad writing.
- **CHAPTER 2** presents 10 principles that will help make your writing crisper and clearer.
- **CHAPTER 3** discusses how to make your writing persuasive and easy to read. It covers writing to the point, building a logical argument and making key information accessible.
- **CHAPTER 4** is about editing – how to make sure your grammar and punctuation are correct while keeping the bigger picture in mind.
- **CHAPTER 5** presents more advanced approaches to make your writing engaging, such as using narrative and varying your style.
- **CHAPTER 6** focuses on how to ensure clear, concise, engaging content in four common writing formats – speeches, opinion pieces, summaries and presentations.

So, let's get started.

CHAPTER 1

Breaking bad habits

All too often writers try to impress rather than inform. This bad habit usually results in writing that is needlessly complex. Why? Because if your priority is to show how much you know and the big words you can use, you will be less concerned about ensuring your reader understands your meaning.

Consider this unfortunate example of South African political-speak:

> The public sector intellectuals and practitioners are currently engaged with finding responses to the pervasive question on whether it is entirely appropriate in all respects, given the difference in circumstances, values and goals between the public and private sectors to have borrowed so heavily from the tools, techniques and approaches of the private sector? ... What we can say without fear of contradiction is the fact that some of the approaches and management techniques that have found its way into the public sector through that paradigmatic shift of thinking that has come over the discipline of public administration, have resulted, to an extent, in improved operational effectiveness. I would like to be so bold as to categorically state that project management is one of the approaches that we have extended to the public sector that have much to offer to our effective functioning. And I can say this even in the knowledge that the full potential thereof have hitherto not been taken advantage of.[1]

South Africa's then-Minister of Public Service and Administration uttered these unmemorable words at a 2003 conference in Johannesburg. This mélange of buzzwords, truisms, jargon and pseudo-intellectual phraseology can thankfully be reduced to its essence as follows:

> As the discipline of public administration has evolved, so have management techniques. Project management approaches, including those borrowed from the private sector, have helped to improve public-sector effectiveness – and we can do more with these tools.

1 Geraldine Fraser-Moleketi, "Project management in the public sector", 26 November 2003.

This example shows how much waffle can be cut away if you care about making your point clearly and concisely.

Even if your subject matter is complex or technical, you can still write about it clearly. What matters is your attitude to the reader. You need to connect with them, sharing what you know rather than making them think, "Wow, this person seems to know so much – but I'm not sure I understand what they're saying."

We often learn by example. Sometimes we learn to write in a way that is suitable for a very limited audience – for example, for your manager or the person who marks your assignments. The same is true if you work in an organisation where all your colleagues, particularly those more senior than you, are determined to sail the seas of jargon.

Take academic writing. It's common for first-year university or college students to get back their initial assignments heavily marked up with their tutor's red ink. And so students quickly learn to write in a more formal way – after all, your marks depend on it! You learn to avoid the first person ("I") and colloquial expressions. You lengthen your sentences and use more academic phrases. You qualify every point you make. You hesitate to voice your own opinions. Your essays become a forest of references. In short, you imitate how your teachers write and, in the process, sacrifice clarity on the altar of complexity.

A major reason academic writing is often unfriendly to the reader is that academics aren't trained to write simply and clearly, nor do they generally care to. As linguist and cognitive psychologist Steven Pinker points out in his article "Why academics stink at writing", they have spent years writing things in a complex way and have been rewarded for doing so.[2] They write for their peers rather than students or non-specialists. If they keep doing this for years and nobody ever challenges them to write more accessibly, there's no incentive for them to change.

This is true not only for academics, but for art critics, engineers, economists, lawyers, policy specialists – in short, anyone who specialises in a complex subject. It's often easier to write in a convoluted way using a lot of jargon than it is to write simply. In some cases, the writer may not fully grasp what they are

2 Steven Pinker, "Why academics stink at writing", *The Chronicle of Higher Education*, 26 September 2014.

writing about and finds it easier to obfuscate than to clarify. It takes time and effort to write clearly; it also requires changing one's attitude so that the reader's understanding comes first.

Fortunately, there are signs of progress. Academic writing published on open access platforms (such as *The Conversation*) needs to be written in accessible language if it's to be understood by a general audience and shared widely.

Sharpening your ability to write clearly will serve you well, whatever your line of work. One of the most valuable intellectual skills is to ask questions – and your questions should extend to how you and those around you communicate. Even if you consider yourself a strong writer, some of the writing habits you formed at school, at university and in the workplace may need to be reconsidered and adjusted.

Let your incentive be this: your readers will be impressed not by how grand you sound but by how clearly you've communicated your ideas – and they will want to read more of your work.

The global standard: Plain language

When we talk about food, "plain" is generally accepted as a euphemism for "flavourless" (more on euphemism later). Many of us prefer things to be tasty rather than bland. But when the topic is technical writing, "plain" is a positive, highly desirable quality. A document written in plain language is one where the content, no matter how complex, will be accessible to a reader who is not an expert in the field.

Globally, there's a trend towards communicating in plain language in business and government. Plain language communications use everyday words and clear sentences to present information in a way that's easy for the reader to understand. This helps make technical or complex subjects accessible for a wide audience. Plain language is becoming increasingly common in fields such as law, insurance and finance, which are trying to shed their reputation for using highfalutin words and complex sentences to confuse, intimidate and exclude. (We'll have more to say about lawyers later, not all of it glowingly appreciative.)

In Australia, Canada, South Africa, the United Kingdom and the United States, plain language is championed in the law. For example, the US Plain Writing Act (2010) requires federal agencies to use clear language to ensure the public can understand what they publish. The US Securities and Exchange Commission's *A Plain English Handbook* (1998) provides guidelines for writing financial disclosures. It notes that the most common problems in disclosure documents are:

- Long sentences
- The passive voice
- Weak verbs
- Unnecessary words and detail
- Legal and financial jargon
- Abstract words
- Unreadable design and layout.

The authors explain that, in contrast to such documents, "[a] plain English document uses words economically and at a level the audience can understand. Its sentence structure is tight. Its tone is welcoming and direct. Its design is visually appealing. A plain English document is easy to read and looks like it's meant to be read."[3] These points underlie the principles of clear writing that we discuss in Chapter 2.

One caveat: *plain* language and *clear* language are not always the same thing. You won't always be able to use plain language, particularly when you're writing about a complex subject. But you should be able to write about any subject, no matter how complex, in a way that is clear. Where plain language is not an option, ensure that your writing is lucid. If you fail this test, you are not communicating.

Transparency and protecting the interests of citizens

Using clear language isn't a matter for arid academic debate: it has real-world consequences. After all, if your key message is lost on your audience – not because they aren't paying attention, but because they can't identify what your message is, or can identify it but can't understand it clearly – then your writing is not fulfilling its purpose. And if the purpose is to inform and prompt action – for example, to advise people of their rights or to explain their income-tax obligations – then the consequences can be serious indeed.

3 Office of Investor Education and Assistance, *A Plain English Handbook*, p. 5.

Using clear language is particularly important in societies marked by high levels of inequality. Unambiguous, lucid writing helps citizens understand and exercise their rights.

In South Africa, the National Credit Act (2005) and the Consumer Protection Act (2008) advocate for plain language because it protects the consumer, particularly the poorer consumer who is at higher risk of exploitation. The consumer protection legislation says that a document is considered to be in plain language:

> if it is reasonable to conclude that an ordinary consumer of the class of persons for whom the notice, document or visual representation is intended, with average literacy skills and minimal experience as a consumer of the relevant goods or services, could be expected to understand the content, significance and import of the notice, document or visual representation without undue effort.[4]

Curiously, this clause takes a wide legal detour around plain language. But leaving aside the unnecessarily complex way it is presented, this passage gets across a valuable idea: all citizens should be able to understand what companies and governments communicate. An organisation risks costly litigation and damage to its reputation if it fails to comply with legislation protecting the rights of consumers.

In a 2012 court case, the Durban High Court ruled in favour of a customer who had purchased (and later returned) a defective vehicle.[5] The court stated that the bank's credit agreement had not sufficiently informed the defendant of his rights and obligations as a consumer, because one or more clauses in the agreement were deceptive.

Organisations need to ensure that consumers can easily understand the terms and conditions in the contracts they sign. Clear language supports transparency and accountability, safeguarding the trust of the reader.

---

4 Government of Republic of South Africa, Consumer Protection Act 68 of 2008, Chapter 2, Part D, subsection 22(2).

5 Standard Bank of South Africa Ltd v Dlamini (2877/2011) [2012] ZAKZDHC 64; 2013 (1) SA 219 (KZD) (23 October 2012). Case report accessed on website of the Southern African Legal Information Institute.

"Transparency" doesn't mean your document should become a data dump, where every last detail is included for fear of leaving something unsaid. One way to lose or confuse your reader is to overwhelm them with information. Transparency, as the word suggests, is about providing *relevant* detail in a way that is clear and meaningful to the reader.

The dead giveaways of bad writing

Bad writing is hard to read and understand. But it's not hard to find. It exhibits some common symptoms, including poor word choice, vagueness, jargon and misuse of punctuation. Here, we'll look at three common problems: wordiness, long sentences and ambiguity.

Wordiness

Verbosity is a virus. And like Covid-19, it has its own nomenclature: circumlocution, garrulousness, logorrhoea, prolixity. Fortunately there is a vaccine, and it's called brevity.

Why use words that lengthen your message without adding value? When we speak, we often emphasise a point with expressions like "and so on and so forth", "each and every one" and "any and all" to no ill effect – but in writing, these same phrases lead to puffy, pompous prose.

Below are some wordy expressions contrasted with concise alternatives.

WORDY	CONCISE
in view of the fact that	given, considering
in the event of	if
in the not-too-distant future	soon
made a statement saying	stated, said
was of the opinion that	thought, believed, said
in the vicinity of	near, close to
take into consideration	consider

The wordy expressions shown above are also stuffier than the alternatives. Beware of overformality, which can sound awkward. Imagine that you're at work on a sweltering day. The air-conditioner is broken. Everyone is short-tempered. Then an email lands.

> Kindly be informed that it has been brought to our attention that the air-conditioning units in the building are not functional. Technicians are currently engaged in repairing the system and envisage that the matter will be resolved by the end of the week. In the interim period, we have sought the use of mobile units to mitigate the current ventilation conditions and are considering the installation of permanent split units to lessen reliance on the centralised system. Please accept our sincere apologies for any inconvenience and discomfort caused.

So though you might crave a cool breeze, windiness will not help. And a phrase like "mitigate the current ventilation conditions" is not just stuffy – it's also abstract. Overly formal language risks leaving your reader confused about what you are trying to say. Wouldn't you prefer this crisper version?

> We apologise for the discomfort caused by the faulty air-conditioning system. Technicians are working on the problem and hope to fix it by the end of the week. In the meantime, we have brought in mobile units and are considering installing split units to reduce the load on the central system.

In war, lives can depend on a clear message. In 1942, during the Second World War, US president Franklin Roosevelt recognised the importance of being specific when he read the following memo:

> Such preparations shall be made as will completely obscure all federal buildings and non-federal buildings occupied by the federal government during an air raid for any period of time from visibility by reason of internal or external illumination.[6]

What do you think government employees were being asked to do? The message doesn't exactly jump out. Which is why Roosevelt responded: "Tell them that in buildings where they have to keep the work going to put something across the windows." The message is clear: obscure the windows (not the message).

6 William Zinsser, *On Writing Well*, p. 8.

Long sentences

Don't test your reader's patience. Sentences that pack in too much information are hard to follow, particularly if punctuation is used improperly. In the following example, in the left-hand column, the reader has to wade through a lot of detail and will struggle to spot the difference between the important and not-so-important points.

TOO MUCH DETAIL, LONG SENTENCE	LESS DETAIL, MORE CONCISE
The International Monetary Fund projects global economic growth of 3.7% in both 2018 and 2019, reflecting a slight downward revision from earlier forecasts as a result of a slowdown in economic activity in some major advanced economies (particularly in the Euro area), the negative effects of escalating global trade tensions, as well as a weaker outlook for some key emerging markets and developing economies arising from country-specific factors, tighter financial conditions, geopolitical tensions, and higher oil import bills.	The International Monetary Fund projects global economic growth of 3.7% in both 2018 and 2019. This reflects a slight downward revision from earlier forecasts. This is due to a slowdown in economic activity in some advanced economies, escalating global trade tensions, and a weaker outlook for key emerging markets and developing economies.

Long sentences often are the result of the writer feeling they need to cram in all the details. When deciding what should stay and what should go, it's vital that as the writer you use your judgement rather than leaving it to the reader to do all the work.

The passive voice also makes for longer sentences. A sentence in the passive voice focuses on the object of an action rather than the actor. Unfortunately, this sometimes leaves the reader wondering who performed the action, as in this sentence: "In the televised debate between the two US presidential candidates, a faux pas was made when Africa was referred to as a country."

Active voice sentences have the virtue of being shorter and more focused. Whereas passive voice sentences either omit the actor or relegate it to the end of the sentence, active voice sentences usually begin with the actor, as shown in the following example.

PASSIVE VOICE	ACTIVE VOICE
Land care and conservation projects focusing on the sustainable use of natural resources have been launched by the department.	The department has launched conservation projects focusing on the sustainable use of natural resources.

If you want to write to the point and show accountability by identifying the agent of an action, use the active voice. We discuss the active voice in more detail in Chapter 2, and in Chapter 5 we demonstrate how to vary your use of the active and passive voice to give your writing optimal flow and focus.

Ambiguity

Murky writing is often the result of unclear thinking and carelessness. Some sentences are confusing because they are ambiguous – they can be interpreted in more than one way. Consider the examples below.

AMBIGUOUS	REVISED
The water and electricity services capital budget is growing at a **declining rate of -60%** over the next three years.	The water and electricity services capital budget is declining at a rate of 60% over the next three years.
Apple unveiled an upgraded smartwatch that can detect heart problems **at its annual product launch event in Cupertino on Wednesday**.	On Wednesday, at its annual product launch event in Cupertino, Apple unveiled an upgraded smartwatch that can detect heart problems.

In the first example, the reader may ask: Is the budget growing or declining? In the second example, the word order suggests that the smartwatch can detect heart problems at the product launch. Apple events are famously exciting, but the organisers wouldn't want any product to be literally heart-stopping to a member of the audience. The problem is solved by simply adjusting the sentence structure.

Don't leave the reader guessing. Say what you mean.

The ingredients of good writing

Good writing considers the reader

Write to be read. This is not as easy as it sounds. Most writing can be read, but often it is not readable – in other words, it's not easy for a reader to make sense of it. You might be an expert in your field, but if you bury your main points in clumsy sentences, overwhelm your reader with inessential detail or stuff your prose with big words that are hard to digest, then you're not doing a good job of connecting with your audience.

Keeping your reader in mind is a key ingredient of good writing. This goes beyond ensuring that your sentences are grammatically correct, as Steven Pinker points out in a 2015 article for *The Guardian*:

> Though bad writing has always been with us, the rules of correct usage are the smallest part of the problem. Any competent copy editor can turn a passage that is turgid, opaque, and filled with grammatical errors into a passage that is turgid, opaque, and free of grammatical errors. Rules of usage are well worth mastering, but they pale in importance behind principles of clarity, style, coherence, and consideration for the reader.[7]

Warren Buffett, one of the world's most successful investors, is a good example of someone who writes with his reader in mind. He is the Chairman and CEO of Berkshire Hathaway, a multinational holding company. A strategy he uses when he writes is to pretend that he's talking to his sisters:

> I have no trouble picturing them: though highly intelligent, they are not experts in accounting or finance. They will understand plain English, but jargon may puzzle them. My goal is simply to give them the information I would wish them to supply me if our positions were reversed. To succeed, I don't need to be Shakespeare; I must, though, have a sincere desire to inform.[8]

---

7 Steven Pinker, "Many of the alleged rules of writing are actually superstitions", *The Guardian*, 6 October 2015.

8 Warren Buffett, Preface to *A Plain English Handbook*, p. 2.

Let's take a look at Buffett's approach. The following example is an extract from his Chairman's letter in 2000 to Berkshire Hathaway shareholders in which he explains the economics of property and casualty insurance. What features make it easy to understand?

> Our core business – though we have others of great importance – is insurance. To understand Berkshire, therefore, it is necessary that you understand how to evaluate an insurance company. The key determinants are: (1) the amount of float that the business generates; (2) its cost; and (3) most critical of all, the long-term outlook for both of these factors.
>
> To begin with, float is money we hold but don't own. In an insurance operation, float arises because premiums are received before losses are paid, an interval that sometimes extends over many years. During that time, the insurer invests the money. This pleasant activity typically carries with it a downside: the premiums that an insurer takes in usually do not cover the losses and expenses it eventually must pay. That leaves it running an "underwriting loss", which is the cost of float. An insurance business has value if its cost of float over time is less than the cost the company would otherwise incur to obtain funds. But the business is a lemon if its cost of float is higher than market rates for money.[9]

The extract contains short, simple sentences and varied use of punctuation. Technical terms are explained in ways that anyone can understand. The tone is direct and conversational, with a touch of humour. The extract still deals seriously with specialised financial terms, but it does so in a way that accommodates a non-specialist reader. (For more concrete guidance on considering your audience, see Chapter 3.)

Good writing is concise

"Brevity is the soul of wit," Shakespeare's Polonius says in *Hamlet* (an ironic remark given that in general Polonius talks far too much). To be concise, you need to strip your sentences down to their essential components. Writing concisely is not easy – it requires discipline and a commitment to clarity. Teju Cole, author of the novel *Open City* (2011), advises one never to use a big word when a small one will do. In his *Eight Letters to a Young Writer* (2010), he notes:

9 Warren Buffett, Chairman's letter, Berkshire Hathaway Annual Report 2000, p. 8.

> There are many who use big words to mask the poverty of their ideas. A straightforward vocabulary, using mostly ordinary words, spiced every now and again with an unusual one, persuades the reader that you're in control of your language. Use simple words fortified by a few bigger ones, and along with this variation, vary, too, the rhythm of your sentences. Most of them should be short, but the occasional long one will give a musical and pleasing cadence to your writing.[10]

A good example of simple words used to great effect is *Things Fall Apart* (1958), which is widely considered Chinua Achebe's masterpiece. The novel tells the story of the demise of a great man, Okonkwo, against the backdrop of the colonial encounter between traditional Igbo society and European missionaries. This is the opening paragraph:

> Okonkwo was well known throughout the nine villages and even beyond. His fame rested on solid personal achievements. As a young man of eighteen he had brought honor to his village by throwing Amalinze the Cat. Amalinze was the great wrestler who for seven years was unbeaten, from Umuofia to Mbaino. He was called the Cat because his back would never touch the earth. It was this man that Okonkwo threw in a fight which the old men agreed was one of the fiercest since the founder of their town engaged a spirit of the wild for seven days and seven nights.[11]

Achebe's sentences are short and to the point. Each word is carefully selected. Adjectives are used sparingly. The passage is informative without being dry. For Achebe, it was important for his narrator to maintain this matter-of-fact tone so that the reader could make their own judgement about the characters.

Concision is as useful for the novelist as it is for the journalist. Here, it's worth mentioning the formative experience of Ernest Hemingway, who had a notably lean writing style that drew on his newspaper experience. After finishing high school in 1917, he worked for six months as a reporter for *The Kansas City Star*. The newspaper's style guide advised journalists: "Use short sentences. Use short first paragraphs. Use vigorous English. Be positive, not negative."[12] These are important first principles that all writers can apply.

---

10 Teju Cole, *Eight Letters to a Young Writer*, p. 6.

11 Chinua Achebe, *Things Fall Apart*, p. 1.

12 Kansas City Star, "The Star Copy Style".

WHAT IS A STYLE GUIDE?

A style guide establishes a consistent framework for written communications. It sets out an organisation's approach to matters of grammar, punctuation, capitalisation, acronyms, terminology, voice, numbers, formatting and similar issues. Such guidelines help to prevent inconsistencies in written communications, and may also cover graphics and branding.

You may not be a journalist or typically need to write anything resembling a news article. Nonetheless, it's worth bearing in mind the purpose of good journalism, which is to inform (not impress) an ordinary reader by conveying relevant information. Whether you are writing a report, a press release or an email – anything to inform or prompt action – it's crucial that your key message is clear and concise.

Good writing is free of jargon

When everyone around you uses big, important-sounding words, it's easy to feel you need to do the same. And so, instead of saying "I'll talk to Sizwe about how we can improve this product", you say "I'm going to reach out to Sizwe to assess how we can optimise this value proposition", which certainly sounds grander.

To avoid dealing with an unpleasant issue, some companies avoid saying they are eliminating jobs. Instead, they serve up an unhealthy mix of jargon and euphemisms, declaring that they are conducting "an orderly ramp-down of about 3,000 persons" or making "investment lay-offs". This type of corporate guff is also used in marketing to exaggerate the qualities of products: for example, when technology entrepreneur Elon Musk says that Tesla is "laser-focused on achieving full self-driving capability on one integrated platform with an order of magnitude greater safety than the average manually driven car".[13]

Linguistic contortions confuse people, particularly where the idea being communicated is not complex. Equally, it's a mistake to assume that complex topics require complex sentences. For example, in a legal contract you might come across a sentence like this:

13 Lucy Kellaway, "Corporate jargon scales new heights", *Financial Times*, 8 January 2017.

> The signatories hereof, being duly authorised thereto, by their signatures hereto authorise the execution of the work detailed herein, or confirm their acceptance of the contents hereof and authorise the implementation/ adoption thereof, as the case may be, for and on behalf of the parties represented by them.

This could just as well be written as, "In signing this document, we authorise the work described here." This plain language version may lack gravitas, but it does have the virtue of being clear and to the point.

Lawyers will argue that legal writing is complicated because it needs to cover all contingencies. Fair enough, but this doesn't need to be accomplished in one very long sentence loaded with Latin phrases, or – to paraphrase Hugh Masekela in a different context – roving, marauding phrases of no particular origin.[14] Since laws apply to us all, we should all be able to understand them – *even* when written by a lawyer.

It's possible to write clearly about complicated matters without sacrificing essential detail. This may involve shortening your sentences, simplifying your language, explaining technical concepts and using devices like bullet points and subheadings. However, doing so requires a shift in approach: to write clearly you need to put your reader's understanding first.

What does it take to become a better writer?

Read widely

It's not easy producing writing that is effortless to read. Professional writers are the first to admit this. The poet Maya Angelou said that to make her writing sound just right: "I try to pull the language into such a sharpness that it jumps off the page. It must look easy, but it takes me forever to get it to look so easy."[15]

---

14 In "Stimela" (Coal Train) (1974), Masekela sings of migrant mineworkers who "think about the loved ones they may never see again / Because they might have already been forcibly removed / From where they last left them / Or wantonly murdered in the dead of night / By roving, marauding gangs of no particular origin".

15 *The Paris Review* 116, Interview: Maya Angelou, The Art of Fiction No. 119 (Autumn 1990).

To become a better writer, you need to read widely and athletically. Read news, blogs and opinion pieces. Read fiction, non-fiction and poetry. Read writing of different genres and by people of diverse backgrounds. Read where your curiosity takes you. As novelist Chimamanda Ngozi Adichie observes, "I'm not sure that one can be a good writer without being a good reader. If you're going to build a desk it's very good to see what other carpenters have done."[16]

If reading brings back bad memories of school, then it's time to create a fresh association. In reading you will discover new worlds, see things from fresh points of view, forget yourself and be reminded of things you've forgotten.

As writer Lebohang Masango reminds us, "Written words will unlock a world of possibilities, if allowed. And possibilities can be abundant!"[17] These possibilities include empowering yourself with knowledge, realising the diversity of human experience and becoming a more skilled communicator.

As you immerse yourself in words, your vocabulary will expand. You'll pick up idioms and turns of phrase that you can use in your own writing.

Imitate and rewrite

A good way to learn is by imitation. But take care to imitate *good* writing habits! The process of writing itself can help you think clearly. How? Well, for words to fit together just right, one often has to try them out in different combinations. In this sense, writing is always a matter of rewriting – whether you're revising as you write or editing a first full draft.

Getting a sentence to sound right is not just about the choice of words but how the sentence gels with those around it. There's always a word that can be changed or added or removed. If you want to be a better writer, be prepared to revise your work extensively. This requires an open, constructive attitude to rewriting. Marvin Swift captures this attitude well:

---

16 From an interview with the *Stylist* Book Club. Quoted in Emily Temple, "Chimamanda Ngozie Adichie on how to write and how to read".

17 Lebohang Masango, "The importance of getting the African youth involved in promoting a culture of reading".

> Rewriting is the key to improved thinking. It demands a real openmindedness and objectivity. It demands a willingness to cull verbiage so that ideas stand out clearly. And it demands a willingness to meet logical contradictions head on and trace them to the premises that have created them. In short, it forces a writer to get up his courage and expose his thinking process to his own intelligence. Obviously, revising is hard work. It demands that you put yourself through the wringer, intellectually and emotionally, to squeeze out the best you can offer. Is it worth the effort? Yes, it is – if you believe you have a responsibility to think and communicate effectively.[18]

Be patient and persist

Many people have a romantic idea of writing that ignores the investment of time and energy that it demands. Make no mistake: writing is an exacting discipline. "Writing is a craft in the way that carpentry is a craft," writes Megan Garber in a piece on Kazuo Ishiguro, winner of the 2017 Nobel Prize in Literature. "There's art to it, sure, and a certain inspiration required of it, definitely, but for the most part you're just sawing and sanding and getting dust in your eyes."[19]

Ishiguro recounts how he wrote the bulk of his masterpiece *Remains of the Day* (1989), a novel about the secret lives of servants, in a four-week period he calls "the crash". During this intensive period, he wrote six days a week, from morning till night, with short breaks for meals. He focused on getting his ideas and words onto the page rather than making them sound perfect. "The priority," Ishiguro says, "was simply to get the ideas surfacing and growing. Awful sentences, hideous dialogue, scenes that went nowhere – I let them remain and ploughed on." This willingness to produce an imperfect first draft and then go back and refine it is a crucial ingredient in becoming a better writer.

As with most skills, developing your writing ability will take time. You won't become a better writer overnight – it's a challenging and rewarding journey that requires you to invest energy and have faith in yourself.

---

18 Marvin H. Swift, "Clear writing means clear thinking means ...", *Harvard Business Review*, no. 73111, January–February 1973, p. 62.

19 Megan Garber, "Writing advice from a (newly minted) Nobel winner", *The Atlantic*, 5 October 2017.

CHAPTER 2

Principles of clear writing

Writing is both an art and a craft. Like the carpenter who needs a measuring tape, a square, a screwdriver and a hammer, the writer also needs the right tools to build sentences, paragraphs and narratives. The 10 principles below, which are applicable in any field, will help you produce clear, compelling writing.

TEN PRINCIPLES OF CLEAR WRITING
1. Be concise 2. Remove needless repetition 3. Write in the active voice 4. Use strong verbs 5. Accentuate the positive 6. Steer clear of jargon 7. Be specific and avoid clichés 8. Craft effective sentences 9. Get your word order right 10. Put the main idea up front

These are guidelines, not commandments. To keep your reader interested, it's important to vary your style – for example, by using short as well as long sentences (more on this in Chapter 5). Sometimes it's more appropriate to use the passive voice than the active voice, or to position the main idea at the end of the sentence for impact. But, in general, if you apply these principles, your writing will be clearer and more engaging.

1. Be concise

In this fast-paced world, attention is at a premium. Even in an office setting, your document will be competing with attention vampires like email, news and social media. So it's vital you capture your reader's attention before it drifts off to Twitter, Instagram or something else. The best way to do this is to ensure that each word in every sentence pulls its weight.

When we speak, we often say:

the reason why is that	***rather than***	because
the question as to whether		whether
there is no doubt but that		no doubt

Look for opportunities to remove unnecessary words. Avoid using phrases like "the fact that" and "the truth is" unless you really do want to emphasise a fact or a truth (as opposed to a lie or a fiction). The same applies to phrases like "in order to" and "with regard to" – use them correctly or they will pad your sentence like cotton wool. Consider the examples below.

WORDY	CONCISE
This is **to a considerable extent** due to …	This is largely due to …
We would like to **call your attention to the fact** that your account is unpaid.	We would like to inform you that your account is unpaid.
There have been fewer new appointments this year **owing to the fact that** the company is restructuring.	There have been fewer new appointments this year because the company is restructuring.
It has come to our attention that all performance reviews submitted over **the course of** the last six months **were effectively incomplete because they omitted key information.**	All performance reviews submitted in the last six months omitted key information.
Table 8 shows key risks that are applicable **to the agricultural sector,** as well as a series of key stakeholders **in this sector.**	Table 8 shows key risks and stakeholders in the agricultural sector.

Wordiness doesn't automatically make a sentence more formal, but it does make it longer, as you can see from comparing these two sentences:

We reached out to the office of the publisher and formally requested confirmation to be provided with the source of the claims made in the article.

We asked the publisher to confirm the source of the claims made in the article.

Wordiness enables other bad habits – like burying the main point at the end of the sentence. Here's an example:

One of the most influential and determining factors of the degree of liberalism of a country's policy on abortion is religion.

To avoid this lengthy letdown of a sentence, recast it with the key term up front and remove the waffle:

Religion has a major influence on the liberalism of a country's abortion policy.

When scanning for wordiness, ask yourself: Which words don't add value? Those are the ones to weed out.

2. Remove needless repetition

Repetition in spoken communication is normal but in writing it comes across as a weakness – unless it is used sparingly for emphasis. In the examples below, the words in bold are repetitive and can be removed.

REPETITIVE	FREE OF REPETITION
In addition, we **also** offer customised products.	We also offer customised products.
It remains unclear how many **net jobs overall** these programmes have generated. The programmes need to be closely monitored and **rigorously evaluated, and their performance assessed** against objectives so that they can **improve and become more cost-effective.**	It remains unclear how many net jobs these programmes have generated. The programmes need to be closely monitored and assessed to become more cost-effective.

Off the back of that inception meeting, an **online working session** will follow. Discussions in **this working session** will help ensure the refinement of proposed activities and timeframes.	There will be an online session after the inception meeting to refine proposed activities and timeframes.
Despite clear **commitments** by **member states**, the capacity of **member states** to handle migration issues does not always allow them to meet their **commitments**.	Member states do not always have the capacity to meet their migration commitments.
Jim had the flu (hereinafter referred to as the "Disease") and went to see Dr Jones (hereinafter referred to as the "Doctor") and the Doctor told Jim that Jim would be better in ten (10) days, provided, however, that (i) Jim stayed home, (ii) Jim drank liquids, and (iii) Jim slept eight (8) hours each night (hereinafter collectively referred to as the "Remedial Conditions") and provided further that if by the expiration of said ten (10) day period and full and complete fulfilment of the Remedial Conditions the Disease was not fully or partially abated to the full and complete satisfaction of the Doctor, in the Doctor's sole and unfettered discretion, then the Doctor would prescribe antibiotics.	Jim had the flu and went to see Dr Jones. The doctor told Jim he would be better in 10 days if he stayed home, drank liquids and slept for eight hours each night. If Jim's condition did not improve by the end of 10 days, the doctor would prescribe antibiotics.

The last example comes to us courtesy of the legal world.[20] Lawyers, of course, are famous for their long-windedness. But in recent years, the movement towards plain language in the law has resulted in greater resistance to legal loquacity. The *Los Angeles Times*, for example, reported as follows on a California court case:

> Judge Alex Kozinski, who serves on the U.S. 9th Circuit Court of Appeals, has had enough of "sly lawyers" who flout court rules with their verbosity. In a mundane order from the court Thursday giving a California state prosecutor permission to file an overly long brief, Kozinski dissented and said he would not read the additional 14 pages. ... "For my part," Kozinski

20 Martin A. Schwartz, "Do you speak legalese?" *The Florida Bar Journal* 91.4 (April 2017).

> said, "I don't feel bound to read beyond the 14,000 words allowed by our rules, so I won't read past page 66 of the state's brief."[21]

Ahem. See principle 1.

Repetition often emerges in a piece of writing that contains a lot of detail. The writer may believe that the repetitive statements help make the points clearer, but, as shown in the examples above, in most cases the repeated phrases can be removed or rephrased to make the sentence less clumsy.

Sometimes it takes skilful editing to avoid repetition. Consider this sentence:

> Life insurance continues to contribute the most towards the total value of new business. It accounts for 86% of the total value of new business.

We obviously want to avoid repeating "the total value of new business". The trick is to ensure that "86%" is positioned next to the words referring to that figure ("the most"). There are at least three possible solutions:

> At 86%, life insurance continues to contribute the most towards the total value of new business.

> Life insurance, at 86%, continues to contribute the most towards the total value of new business.

> Life insurance continues to contribute the most (86%) towards the total value of new business.

The third version is strongest because the extra information in brackets doesn't break the flow of the sentence. It's generally not difficult to trim repetition from a sentence, but it does take some time and attention. Consider everything you write to be a first draft until you've looked it over again, weeded out unnecessary words and tightened the focus.

Avoid redundancy

Redundancy occurs when you use two or more words that have a similar meaning. In the following examples, just one of the two words is needed:

---

21 Maura Dolan, "Federal judge is fed up with verbose lawyers and their bloated briefs", *Los Angeles Times*, 4 August 2016.

- End result
- Added bonus
- Advance planning
- New innovation
- Cooperate together.

Of course, there may be situations where, for example, you speak about a preliminary result, a secondary result and an *end* result – but then the various types of result need to be specified.

The phrase "going forward" is a particular problem. Like an ingrown toenail, it turns on itself, as in "Our company will grow going forward". But growth can only happen as time progresses, so it's enough to say "Our company will grow".

REDUNDANT	FREE OF REDUNDANCY
The context for this paper **is informed** by socio-economic conditions in South Africa.	This paper is informed by socio-economic conditions in South Africa.
The **new** outreach centre **built this year** is **in close proximity to** the grassroots community, allowing a **faster response time** and **more effective and productive** interventions.	The new outreach centre is close to the community, allowing for faster and more effective interventions.

Repetition for emphasis

Repeating a point – ideally, at the end of a piece and in slightly different words – can be a good way to drive home your message. In *The Everlasting Story of Nory* (1998), Nicholson Baker uses repetition to create rhythm, emphasis and humour:

> Nory was a Catholic because her mother was a Catholic, and Nory's mother was a Catholic because her father was a Catholic, and her father was a Catholic because his mother was a Catholic, or had been.[22]

22 Nicholson Baker, *The Everlasting Story of Nory*, chapter 11.

The repetition gives us the sense of unthinking imitation by the characters. In spoken presentations, repeating certain points can help a listener follow the thread of a speech and remember the main themes. Artful repetition is a staple feature of former US president Barack Obama's speeches. Below is an extract from the speech he delivered in Johannesburg in July 2018 on the centenary of Nelson Mandela's birth. Notice how he emphasises the words "I believe":

> Let me tell you what I believe. I believe in Nelson Mandela's vision. I believe in a vision shared by Gandhi and [Martin Luther] King and Abraham Lincoln. I believe in a vision of equality and justice and freedom and multi-racial democracy, built on the premise that all people are created equal, and they're endowed by our creator with certain inalienable rights. And I believe that a world governed by such principles is possible and that it can achieve more peace and more cooperation in pursuit of a common good. That's what I believe.[23]

So, repetition has its uses. But unless you're using it deliberately and skilfully for emphasis, try to avoid it or edit it out: there's an excellent chance your writing will be leaner and stronger without it.

3. Write in the active voice

The active voice tends to make sentences shorter, more robust, engaging and – yes – more active. In an active voice sentence, the subject of the sentence performs the action. For example, "Bongiwe opened a savings account." Here, Bongiwe is the subject and "opened" is the verb. In contrast, in a passive voice sentence the subject is what is acted upon, as in "A savings account was opened by Bongiwe".

Passive voice sentences often fail to specify who or what is doing the action, as in "Your report has been noted". Frustratingly, of course, we do not know who has noted the report. To translate this into the active voice, you need to know who performed the action; a solution could be "We have noted your report". Active voice sentences are shorter and more direct than passive voice sentences and help to show accountability (who is responsible for an action).

23 Barack Obama, "2018 Nelson Mandela Annual Lecture", 17 July 2018.

Consider the examples below (the verbs in bold are in the passive voice).

PASSIVE	ACTIVE
Two people **were hired** by the company.	The company hired two people.
The production of growth estimates by the economic analysis division **needs to be done** before hiring plans **can be assessed** by the committee.	The economic analysis division needs to produce growth estimates before the committee can assess hiring plans.
The road **was crossed** by the chicken.	The chicken crossed the road.

As the chicken example shows, for a sentence to be in the active voice, there doesn't always need to be a human agent present. It's worth bearing this in mind when you're referring to things like a table, figure, graphic, chapter or section.

PASSIVE	ACTIVE
A summary of the risks **is provided in Figure 2.**	Figure 2 summarises the risks.
The project's background, rationale and methodology **are outlined** in this section.	This section outlines the project's background, rationale and methodology.

Sentences in the active voice are generally more direct and robust. They omit passive constructions like "there were" or "it emerged" and get to the point quicker. Notice the crisp combination of subject and verb that begins each of the active voice sentences below: "People flocked", "Spring arrived", "The storm brought", "The survey shows". This is what makes these sentences more vigorous and concise.

PASSIVE	ACTIVE
The beaches were where most people headed in the good weather.	People flocked to the beaches in the good weather.
The arrival of spring was sooner than expected this year.	Spring arrived early this year.
Accompanying the storm were heavy rain and high winds.	The storm brought a downpour and high winds.
The indications from the survey are that solar power is emerging as a more popular option in cities.	The survey shows that solar power is becoming more popular in cities.

When is the passive voice appropriate?

The passive voice is generally more appropriate if the agent of an action is unknown or less important. Some examples:

A parcel arrived.

A warrant has been issued for his arrest.

Questions were raised at the meeting about how to evaluate progress.

It can be useful if you want to focus attention on the object of an action rather than the action itself: "Bureaucratese is easy to make fun of but a hard habit to shake." The passive voice is also a handy way of being polite or diplomatic. For example, "I noticed the biscuits were finished and not replaced" is more polite and impersonal than "You finished the biscuits and didn't replace them".

Passive voice as a means of evading responsibility

When it comes to admitting responsibility for mistakes, few politicians and company executives are bold enough to use the active voice. Far more common is an evasive statement in the passive voice that doesn't specify the kind of mistakes that were made or who made them.

"Mistakes have been made" is how the CEO of auditing firm KPMG South Africa, Trevor Hoole, admitted in August 2017 to the company's role in the state capture corruption scandal that implicated former president Jacob Zuma and his close allies. The active voice is part of what makes Hoole's next sentence only slightly more credible.

> We commit to take every action necessary to apply these learnings to strengthen the way we work and help restore the public trust we have earned ...[24]

Crucially, the active voice enables readers to hold the writer accountable for their statements.

Tracking readability

Microsoft Word has a function that measures readability. Among other things, it shows the percentage of passive sentences, which usually means a greater number of long sentences. You can activate the function as part of the spelling and grammar check.

This feature also calculates the total number of words, sentences and paragraphs in the document, and the average number of characters per word, words per sentence and sentences per paragraph. However, bear in mind that a readability index is a limited measure of how easy it is to understand your writing. Take this example:

> While the official unemployment rate remained around 29% during 2019, the broad unemployment rate increased slightly from 40.9% to 41.4% through the year.

If you think that your readers may not understand the term "broad unemployment rate", you may need to add a short definition in another sentence, such as:

> Unlike the official unemployment rate, the broad rate includes discouraged work-seekers who are no longer actively looking for a job.

Adding an explanation might negatively affect the readability calculations, but in this case it helps improve the reader's understanding, which is more important. It's up to you as the writer to judge whether it's necessary to explain a term or concept for your intended audience.

---

24 Genevieve Quintal, "KPMG acts against three partners over Gupta leaks disclosures", *TimesLive*, 11 August 2017.

4. Use strong verbs

English is full of wonderful verbs. Use them to make your sentences active and direct.

Let's have a look at strong verbs at work. In the table on the facing page, there are two passages – one original, one modified – placed side by side. They contain the same content but slightly different phrasing. Look particularly at the phrases highlighted in bold on the left and underlined on the right. One of the passages – can you guess which? – is from Njabulo Ndebele's novel *The Cry of Winnie Mandela* (2003).

The phrasing in passage 1 is not less clear or less readable than in passage 2, but it is longer and more roundabout. The phrasing in passage 2 is more vigorous and direct. We hope you guessed it: passage 2 was written by Ndebele. His skilled use of verbs and simple language are signature features of his writing, which includes novels, short stories, poetry, essays, speeches and reviews. His work is influential and has earned him wide acclaim – not just because it is insightful but because he communicates in a way that is clear and accessible.

Alas, many a healthy verb has been crippled by being turned into a noun. Nominalisation, as this disreputable practice is known, spreads like wildfire. The noun form of a verb is longer and lends itself to passive sentences. So, wherever possible, use the verb rather than its noun form.

NOUN FORM OF VERB	VERB
arrangement	arrange
completion	complete
provision	provide
participation	participate
development	develop
realisation	realise

PASSAGE 1	PASSAGE 2
Strong pressures to leave his family of five children **are what finally prompt the departure of** Lejone Mofolo.	Lejone Mofolo finally yields to strong pressures to leave his family of five children.
He does not **want to be a helpless observer** as the world collapses around him.	He cannot just sit back and watch the world collapse around him.
There is drought.	Drought.
The deep highlands of Lesotho have **not been visited by** rain for many years.	The deep highlands of Lesotho have seen no rain for many years.
People have been asked by the King to pray for rain, but God, remaining as silent as the clear burning skies, **has not deigned to respond.**	The King has called for prayers, but God, remaining as silent as the clear burning skies, has simply not responded.
The role of a man in this world is to ensure that his wife and children **are cared for.**	A man has to take care of his wife and children.
It is necessary that he provides his family with food, **puts clothes on their backs**, and **ensures that they are able to take shelter within the sturdy walls of a house that he has built with his own hands.**	A man has to feed his family, buy them clothes, and build a decent house for them.
The maize has been devastated by drought.	Drought has killed all the maize.
Yet, Lejone goes to the fields **on a regular basis, certain in the knowledge that** he will find nothing but the dry sods turned up at the last planting season.	Yet, Lejone goes to the fields frequently, knowing he will find nothing but the dry sods turned up at the last planting season.
Some maize shoots, in their early enthusiasm for life, had **managed to find a way to push the sods aside** with their tiny, surprisingly strong stems and **emerge into the light and fresh air,** reaching out to the sun.	Some maize shoots, in their early enthusiasm for life, had pushed sods aside with their surprisingly strong, tiny stems, reaching out to the sun.[25]

25 Njabulo Ndebele, *The Cry of Winnie Mandela*, p. 8.

Take another look at the table on page 32. To use the nouns in the left column, you would need to introduce yet another verb, as in "I will ensure the completion of the assignment", versus "I will complete the assignment". This clumsy process is illustrated in the table below. The verb-centred sentences on the right are shorter and more concise than the noun-heavy ones on the left.

USING LONG NOUN PHRASES	USING VERBS
I must **make an application** for funding.	I must apply for funding.
When would be a good time to **have a discussion** about the proposal?	When would be a good time to discuss the proposal?
We must **undertake the analysis** of new data for the briefing.	We must analyse new data for the briefing.
The committee is responsible for the: • **Implementation of** ... • **Reprioritisation of** ... • **Facilitation of** ... • **Reduction of** ...	The committee will: • Implement ... • Reprioritise ... • Facilitate ... • Reduce ...

Becoming a better writer requires you to appreciate the suppleness of language. As with technical jargon, bland buzzwords like "development", "service delivery", "realisation of goals" and "resource management" tend to be used without thinking. It's easy to forget that these nouns can be turned into verbs and used in active voice sentences to reduce wordiness.

NOUN PHRASES	REVISED WITH VERBS
These offices are responsible for helping municipalities with **the identification** and **development of** viable market opportunities.	These offices are responsible for helping municipalities identify and develop viable market opportunities.
Your responsibilities include **the preparation of** surveys and **the evaluation of** user feedback.	Your responsibilities include preparing surveys and evaluating user feedback.

We are **undertaking the creation of** an implementation plan to help the department **realise effective and efficient service delivery.**	We are creating a plan to help the department deliver services effectively and efficiently.

Break up noun stacks

A noun stack – a clump of nouns in close succession – can clutter a sentence and slow its flow. The writer who builds such a disreputable stack often intends to save space but ends up causing confusion. For example, "Failed password security question answer attempts limit" is impenetrable. It would be more reader-friendly if we wrote it out as "Limit reached on attempts to answer security question for failed password". Noun stacks commonly occur in newspaper headlines and can be difficult to parse, like this bizarre example: "Corpse sex kill threat prisoner gets 45 year sentence".[26]

We leave it to you to figure that one out.

Although grammatically correct, the sentences below on the left are hard to read. To remove the noun stacks (in bold), you need to convert key nouns to verbs, insert verbs and prepositions, and shuffle the word order.

NOUN STACKS	BREAKING UP NOUN STACKS
The project involves **conflict systems analysis handbook preparation.**	The project involves preparing a handbook on analysing conflict systems.
There will be an **employee community involvement information session** on Tuesday.	On Tuesday, there will be an information session on community involvement for employees.
This report focuses on **provincial Public Works residential rental stock.**	This report focuses on residential rental stock owned by provincial Public Works departments.

26 "Noun pile of the week", Language Log, 14 December 2016, and "Corpse sex kill threat prisoner gets 45 year sentence", Nehanda Radio, 15 December 2016.

As Khumalo raced down the open field, a sudden **waistband elastic integrity malfunction** led to a **shorts position departure event,** causing a **balance impairment-induced score denial.**	As Khumalo raced down the open field, his waistband snapped, his shorts fell and he face-planted onto the pitch, denying him a goal.

Dr Seuss's *Fox in Socks* (1965) provides a fun illustration of what happens when you take a clearly formulated clause containing the necessary articles (the, a), verbs and prepositions, and turn it into a noun stack: "When beetles fight these battles in a bottle with their paddles and the bottle's on a poodle and the poodle's eating noodles, they call this a muddle puddle tweetle poodle beetle noodle bottle paddle battle."[27]

5. Accentuate the positive

"You got to ac-cen-tchu-ate the positive," sang Ella Fitzgerald (and many others). Words worth remembering. If you want to state an idea directly, use positive terms rather than negative ones. As with the active voice, a positive formulation is generally shorter. So, instead of being indirect and saying:

> Without deviating from the terms and conditions of the competition, the judging panel decided not to award prizes in any of the categories except two.

be direct and say:

> In line with the terms and conditions of the competition, the judging panel decided to award prizes in only two categories.

Here are some examples of indirect phrases compared with direct alternatives.

27 Dr Seuss, *Fox in Socks.*

INDIRECT (BY NEGATION)	DIRECT (POSITIVE STATEMENT)
does not have	lacks
does not include	excludes
not able	unable
not present	absent
not certain	uncertain
not the same	different
not many	few
not often on time	usually late rarely on time

As with the active and passive voice, different occasions call for different approaches. The negative is preferable if the writer wants to stress what is not the case or not allowed. Some examples:

> It is not advisable to spend more money than you earn.
>
> Food and drinks are not allowed on the train.
>
> Fraud and other forms of dishonesty will not be tolerated.
>
> After your first visit, you are not required to sign in.

Or you may want to take the edge off a critical opinion. "I think browsing Facebook is not a sensible use of time" is politer than "I think browsing Facebook is a waste of time". If you want to moderate the impact of your opinion, choose your words carefully.

Indirectness is useful for being diplomatic. There's a big difference in tone between "We have rejected your application" (blunt) and "We regret to inform you that your application on this occasion was not successful" (courteous). If, on the other hand, you want to firmly express your dissatisfaction with a product, you'd be better off saying "I'm dissatisfied with this product" rather than "This product has not lived up to my expectations".

The double negative occasionally has its uses. But it's best avoided where it's likely to confuse the reader or create awkward phrasing. Consider the following.

CONFUSING DOUBLE NEGATIVE	CLEARER POSITIVE FORMULATION
We have been reliably informed that **optimism** that the bans on the sale of alcohol and tobacco will be lifted **is not misplaced.**	We have been reliably informed that the bans on the sale of alcohol and tobacco are likely to be lifted.
Requests for reflective bibs keep flooding in and **we do not want to not respond** to requests.	Requests for reflective bibs keep flooding in and we want to respond to all requests.
The political party said it would take to task its members who **voted against** an amendment **bill that bars** marriage officials from **refusing** to marry same-sex couples.	The political party said it would discipline its members who voted against an amendment bill that requires officials to marry same-sex couples if requested.

Generally, instead of saying what you don't want to do (or what you don't want to *not* do), say what you *do* want to do.

6. Steer clear of jargon

Jargon is specialised language used by people in a particular field. It can be a quick way of communicating with those who share your knowledge but, used thoughtlessly, it can exclude those who aren't familiar with the details of a subject. Consider this sentence:

> The report proposes a battery of cohort studies to investigate causality and comorbidities in coronavirus patients.

In the medical field, technical terms such as cohort (a group that is part of a clinical trial or study and is observed over a period of time), causality (the relationship between cause and effect) and comorbidity (more than one disease or condition being present in the same person at the same time) are well understood. Not so much to those who haven't studied medicine!

If you were writing about this subject for a non-medical audience, you would need to find a way to express it without the technical terms. For example:

> The report proposes a series of clinical trials to investigate cause and effect, and the presence of more than one disease or condition, in coronavirus patients.

Jargon is common in marketing, where it swims in soupy camaraderie with buzzwords and clichés, and the goal is to convince someone who knows nothing about a product or service that it's worth spending money on. Here's an example of marketing-speak:

> Our mission is to solution the customer holistically.

Presumably, few of us would want to be solutioned holistically, particularly if we don't know what the "solutioning" involves. A plainer version may sound less sexy but has the virtue of being specific and understandable:

> We aim to meet our customers' needs.

Catchy press statements are also often difficult to understand. In January 2020, Warner Bros. announced it would be introducing a project management system driven by artificial intelligence that would "inform decision-making around content and talent valuation to support release strategies". In other words, Warner Bros. will use artificial intelligence to help it decide what movies to make.[28]

Status anxiety is often a factor in the careless use of jargon. Some writers assume that the more obscure and sophisticated they sound, the more they will impress their audience. This tendency is common in academia and politics, and most other professional spheres. And so you might come across a sentence like this, where the terms in bold inflate the importance:

> The report makes **deep dives** on the question of **optimal methodologies** that the city can adopt to **streamline and integrate its utilisation** of water resources.

Deep diving seems to be a popular sport these days, particularly in government and the corporate sector. In the above example, although we're not talking about an ocean-going vessel, "streamline" is in keeping with the water theme – but

---

28 Steve Rose, "'It's a war between technology and a donkey' – how AI is shaking up Hollywood", *The Guardian*, 16 January 2020.

then why use "integrate" as well? The author has chosen to use more, big words rather than a few accurate ones. A jargon-free translation would look like this:

> The report examines how the city can best use its water resources.

This version is less of a mouthful and the loss of guff is a gain in clarity. Often, the use of jargon corrupts the sentence in other ways – verbs become nouns, passive is preferred over the active voice, the sentence gets longer and the logical thread is lost. See for yourself:

> My penultimate proposal relates to the criticality of having stable employment and community relations. Partnership with the trade union movement to sustainably grow the mining sector and continue to improve health and safety are important.[29]

Let's look at three problems that stem from the impulse to use jargon here.

1. **AMBIGUITY**: Is the opening statement the writer's proposal or does the proposal *relate to* this statement? The way this is written suggests that if there is indeed a proposal, it's vague.
2. **NOMINALISATION**: "the criticality of". That sounds very strange. You wouldn't say, "The criticality of brushing your teeth in the morning." Keep it simple: "it is critical to".
3. **LOSS OF LOGICAL THREAD**: "Partnership with ... to grow and to improve ... are important." *Partnership* is the subject of the sentence but the succession of to's and and's, which help pack in the detail, lead to the plural "are", indicating that the writer has forgotten the focus of the sentence. It's easy to lose the thread of what you're saying when you're more focused on showcasing big words and providing too much detail.

We could rewrite that example as follows:

> It is critical to have stable employment and community relations. Developing a partnership with trade unions to sustainably grow the mining sector, and improve health and safety, can complement these broader goals.

---

29 Roger Baxter, "Crucial for SA to focus on leadership compact to effect structural reform", *Business Day*, 3 June 2020.

Politicians are accustomed to using formal language punctuated by vaulting phrases. But if their audience is the general public and their purpose is to inform, then it's fitting to speak plainly so that citizens will understand. During the Covid-19 pandemic, the South African president, Cyril Ramaphosa, delivered televised national updates on the crisis. In a TV interview after one speech, he spoke about the possibility of the ban on tobacco products being lifted on a lower Covid-19 alert level. "We are going to migrate to another level," he said. "Those who are hankering for tobacco must know that it is only a matter of time before their hankering is assuaged or addressed." Note the old-fashioned word "hanker" (which means to want) and the redundancy of "assuaged or addressed", which are effectively synonyms in this case. He could have said, "We hope to move to level 2 soon when people will be able to buy cigarettes."[30] But the elevated diction came more naturally to him.

This example shows how a manner of speaking can become easily ingrained if everyone around you speaks in that way. But it also underlines the very real consequences of misjudging your language. There will always be people who admire the elevated rhetoric of politicians, but during a pandemic these admirers will be massively outnumbered by those wanting to understand the words addressed to them by the president on national TV. If those words go over your head, you might keep the TV on, but you will almost certainly tune out.

It's no good writing in a way that loses your reader. Take the example of "Brexit", a term that came into being in 2016 when 52% of voters in a British referendum decided that the United Kingdom should leave the European Union. Brexit was widely covered in the United Kingdom, and it can be assumed that people who followed the ups and downs of the subsequent negotiations were familiar with the term. The same was not necessarily true for readers who did not live with this term on a daily basis. Note how the term was briefly explained in the excerpt below, which appeared in the *New York Times*:

> In a last-ditch effort to try to get Parliament to pass her plan for Britain to leave the European Union, [former] Prime Minister Theresa May on Wednesday offered to step down and allow another prime minister who has the confidence of her party and lawmakers to negotiate the final

30 Ian Glenn, "Should President Ramaphosa fire his speechwriters?" News24.com, 7 June 2020.

> details. Mrs. May's stunning overture to her fellow Conservatives came just as Parliament tried to sideline her and come up with its own plan for Brexit, as the process of leaving the bloc is known.[31]

A passing explanation like this doesn't take much extra effort on the part of the writer, but it can mean the difference between leaving an uninformed reader none the wiser and drawing that reader into a community of shared understanding. Equally, when a term like "Brexit" has gained wide currency, it's important to use it – rather than avoiding it – to activate the knowledge about it that many people already have.

What if you work in a field where technical terms can't be avoided – like biotechnology or financial services? The same principle applies: consider your reader. Where possible and appropriate, explain technical terms in clear language so that they are meaningful to those unfamiliar with them. The following examples show how you can include a brief explanation between dashes, commas or brackets.

TECHNICAL TERMS	WITH A BRIEF EXPLANATION
In 2018, our **return on equity** was 16.4%.	In 2018, our return on equity – which measures profitability for shareholders – was 16.4%.
CRISPR was recently used by a Chinese scientist to genetically modify human embryos, which were transferred to the egg-donor and resulted in the birth of twins. The announcement of the procedure caused intense debate around the ethics of gene editing of **germline cells**, particularly as this can alter genes that are passed on to the next generation, thereby modifying the human gene pool.	CRISPR, a gene-editing technology, was recently used by a Chinese scientist to genetically modify human embryos, which were transferred to the egg-donor and resulted in the birth of twins. The announcement of the procedure led to intense debate on the ethics of gene editing of human eggs, sperm or embryos (also known as germline cells). Such changes can alter genes that are passed on to the next generation, thereby modifying the human gene pool.

31 Stephen Castle, "Alternate Brexit plans rejected; Theresa May offers to step down", *New York Times*, 28 March 2019.

Often, technical terms are used in perfectly grammatical sentences, like this:

> The self-storage property sector offers diversified income with real asset underpin that is defensive in nature.

The problem is that most of us won't know that "diversified income" means lots of small tenants; "real asset underpin" means that if a tenant doesn't pay, their stored property can be sold; and "defensive in nature" means that consumers tend to cling to possessions. There's nothing in the sentence to help you make sense of it. Clarifying the meaning may require recasting the sentence. So, a sentence like this:

> The global economic recovery is subject to a range of downside risks and potential headwinds.

could be adjusted to this:

> Although the global economy is recovering, a range of risks still threaten growth.

You can't expect someone unfamiliar with financial terminology to know what headwinds are (no, they don't have anything to do with aviation in this case). But you can help them understand by rephrasing your point in simpler terms. Another approach would be to follow the original sentence with some examples to illustrate your meaning. For instance:

> Trade tensions, especially between the United States and its trading partners, have negatively affected the world economy. The lasting effects of national lockdowns to contain the spread of Covid-19 pose further threats to growth.

Similarly, when you use a term like "stakeholders", bear in mind that not all readers will know who you are referring to. To get around this problem, you obviously don't need to name every stakeholder, but it can be helpful to give a representative range, introduced with "such as" or "including". For example, "Our Annual General Meeting is open to all our stakeholders, from investors and donors to partner organisations and clients."

Finally, beware of jargon from the administrative-political realm. One example is the term "employment opportunities", as in the encouraging statement that is not quite a promise: "We aim to create more employment opportunities." That's more jobs, right? Wrong. That's more opportunities to be involved in work that may lead to a job with a wage or salary. It may be an apprenticeship or an internship or a training course or a job-shadowing position. It's an opportunity, not a job.

The slippery use of a term like this – usually by politicians – is often deliberate and serves to obscure rather than clarify. If you mean jobs, then say "jobs". If you want to hedge your commitment like a politician or a bureaucrat, then say "employment opportunities". But beware of thinking that the two are interchangeable. You wouldn't want to turn up on your first day of work somewhere and learn the unpleasant news that you won't be getting paid for the work. Similarly, be straight with your reader and say what you mean. Trust us: it'll pay off.

7. Be specific and avoid clichés

Use concrete language

"High-quality learning environments for children are a necessary precondition for facilitation and enhancement of the learning process." Really? If the point is that "Children need good schools if they are to learn properly", then why not simply say so?

To be specific in your descriptions and examples, you need to convey concrete information. You will inevitably resort to jargon and vagueness if you don't have the necessary detail to paint a rich picture. Here's what Strunk and White, the authors of that classic text on clear writing *The Elements of Style* (first edition published in 1959), have to say on the matter:

> If those who have studied the art of writing are in accord on any one point, it is this: the surest way to arouse and hold the reader's attention is by being specific, definite, and concrete. The greatest writers – Homer, Dante, Shakespeare – are effective largely because they deal in particulars and report the details that matter. Their words call up pictures.[32]

---

32 William Strunk, Jr, and E.B. White, *The Elements of Style*, p. 21.

It's reassuring to know that vague, abstract writing is not just produced by inexperienced writers. In fact, some of the most frequent offenders are professionals who use sophisticated-sounding vocabulary that lacks specificity.

In 2015, two academics, Franco Moretti and Dominique Pestre, published a study analysing 65 years of the World Bank's annual reports. They identified a rise in what they call "management discourse" or "bank speak" and a decline in factual precision. They noted an increased use of jargon and acronyms, fewer references to specific timeframes and a tendency to turn verbs into nouns, leading to more passive voice sentences. To illustrate their point, Moretti and Pestre presented an extract from a 1958 World Bank report. Notice how the passage refers to many concrete details:

> The Congo's present transport system is geared mainly to the export trade, and is based on river navigation and on railroads which lead from river ports into regions producing minerals and agricultural commodities. Most of the roads radiate short distances from cities, providing farm-to-market communications. In recent years road traffic has increased rapidly with the growth of the internal market and the improvement of farming methods.[33]

The authors then presented a contrasting extract from a 2008 World Bank report:

> Countries in the region are emerging as key players on issues of global concern, and the Bank's role has been to support their efforts by partnering through innovative platforms for an enlightened dialogue and action on the ground, as well as by supporting South-South cooperation.

Notice how general this second example is. It's full of smooth-sounding but vague terms like "key players", "issues of global concern", "innovative platforms", "enlightened dialogue" and "action on the ground". The "ground" and the "platforms" here are too abstract for the reader to stand on. Take another look at that sentence: its meaning, if it ever had a clear meaning, evaporates into thin air.

---

33 Franco Moretti and Dominique Pestre, "Bankspeak", pp. 75–76.

Abstain from the instant soup of clichés

Clichés and vague statements are close cousins. A cliché is an expression that has lost its spark through overuse. Some can be amusing, and they are often visually appealing and easy to remember. It's common to use clichés when you're speaking, but in writing they come across as stale. Like instant soup, they are quick and easy to use but also a sign of laziness and lack of originality. If you want your writing to be distinct, rather formulate a fresh turn of phrase.

Here's a sentence packed with clichés (in bold):

> The **sad truth** is that some organisations are not open to **out-of-the-box** approaches to problem-solving. The support of a champion might make all the difference, as this person might be able to **open closed doors** and **level the playing field** by engaging with directors who are not accustomed to **listening to other people's two cents**.

There are various ways to interpret a cliché like *thinking out of the box*. You could mean creative, unconventional, innovative or simply different. That's why clichés can undermine clarity – because you're leaving it to the reader to work out what you mean. Revising the above passage so it's free of clichés could leave us with:

> Some organisations resist creative approaches to solving problems, partly because directors are not accustomed to considering staff initiatives. In such cases, fresh ideas need a champion who can share employees' ideas with management.

Now, it's good to be specific – but don't overwhelm your reader with too much detail. Avoid the kitchen-sink approach. Rather focus on *relevant* detail. Here's a mouthful of a sentence to avoid:

> Training at the grassroots level will focus on capacity building to mobilise public leadership to engage robustly with office bearers in the fields of human rights and crime prevention such as civil servants, government commissions on human rights and the relevant ministries.

There are too many words in this sentence. Too much cud to chew. Careful phrasing gives us a more appetising version:

> Training will help community leaders work closely with state agencies responsible for upholding human rights and preventing crime.

Using clichés in your writing can encourage other kinds of mental laziness – like using stereotypes. A stereotype collapses something specific and unique into a flat generic version. Binyavanga Wainaina's "advice" in his blisteringly funny essay "How to write about Africa" (first published in 2006) plays up some of the stock images that often feature in writing about Africa:

> In your text, treat Africa as if it were one country. It is hot and dusty with rolling grasslands and huge herds of animals and tall, thin people who are starving. Or it is hot and steamy with very short people who eat primates. Don't get bogged down with precise descriptions. Africa is big: fifty-four countries, 900 million people who are too busy starving and dying and warring and emigrating to read your book. The continent is full of deserts, jungles, highlands, savannahs and many other things, but your reader doesn't care about all that, so keep your descriptions romantic and evocative and unparticular.[34]

Beware of clichés of the imagination. Most of us, for example, cherish freedom of speech. Exercising that right may involve speaking or writing one's mind without regard to the powers that be, or challenging accepted norms. Such acts may require different degrees of courage or chutzpah. But not every such utterance is "speaking truth to power". This phrase, through overuse, has become a stale marketing blurb. You may be challenging some injustice, trying to retire an outdated practice, carving out a new cultural space or writing about a technical problem. Whatever the case, choose fresh words and images. The well-chosen word or phrase can light a fire; a cliché is a damp match.

So, avoid the instant soup of stereotypes and clichés, which are high in bulk but low in value. Instead, be specific and include relevant detail: it will make your writing more nutritious, easier to digest and truer to reality.

---

34 Binyavanga Wainaina, "How to write about Africa", *Granta* 92, 2 May 2019.

8. Craft effective sentences

To be effective, a sentence needs to be complete, it needs to make sense and it needs to propel the reader safely to the next sentence. Think of sentences in a text as planks nailed down side by side and designed to support the weight of a person walking over them. They need to hang together to form a sturdy structure. A faulty sentence, like a rotten plank on a bridge strung across a gorge, is a hazard to the unsuspecting reader.

A complete sentence may consist of just one word (Help! Go! Yes!) or a few (Not now. Maybe later.) or many. Completeness is not about the number of words but whether the sentence is *grammatically* coherent. In this section we're going to focus on sentences that are not grammatically complete because they are missing information or words, or contain an awkward surplus of one or the other.

Sentence fragments

A sentence fragment is a sentence that is grammatically incomplete, usually because it's one half of a longer sentence that has been incorrectly split in two. Fragments need to be integrated with their other half with a suitable punctuation mark or reworded so they can stand alone. A comma does the trick of completing the fragments (in bold) in the examples below.

SENTENCE FRAGMENT	COMPLETE SENTENCE
The company has established offices in a further five countries. **A way of broadening its reach on the continent.**	The company has established offices in a further five countries, broadening its reach on the continent.
Our citizenship approach has evolved over a number of years. **A shift from philanthropy to a more business-led approach that considers the broader impact we can have on society.**	Our citizenship approach has evolved over a number of years, shifting from philanthropy to a more business-led approach that considers the broader impact we can have on society.

There are times when a very short sentence can work well alongside a longer one. Take this example:

> After months of planning, training and consulting with nutrition and physical conditioning experts, the team is focusing its efforts on a long-held dream. To win!

Here, it's clear that the two-word sentence is the capstone to the longer one: there is no need for a colon or a dash. The difference in sentence length only helps to vary the rhythm, making it more engaging to read.

There's a place for the sentence fragment and the deliberately long sentence, especially in fiction. Charles Dickens begins his novel *Bleak House* (1852–53) with a series of evocative sentence fragments. Here are the first few:

> London. Michaelmas Term lately over, and the Lord Chancellor sitting in Lincoln's Inn Hall. Implacable November weather. As much mud in the streets as if the waters had but newly retired from the face of the earth, and it would not be so wonderful to meet a Megalosaurus, forty feet long or so, waddling like an elephantine lizard up Holborn Hill. Smoke lowering down from chimney-pots, making a soft black drizzle, with flakes of soot in it as big as full-grown snow-flakes – gone into mourning, one might imagine, for the death of the sun. Dogs, undistinguishable in mire. Horses, scarcely better; splashed to their very blinkers.

Some of these sentences are not short, but they are all fragments. And as fragments they work as a series of snapshots setting the scene.

The extra-long sentence has also been put to good use by novelists. The Irish writer Mike McCormack's 2016 novel *Solar Bones* consists of a single sentence that runs on for more than 270 pages. This daring approach won the author the Goldsmiths Prize and the 2018 International Dublin Literary Award. His more famous compatriot James Joyce ends his acclaimed novel *Ulysses* (1919) with the main character's wife, Molly Bloom, delivering an unpunctuated soliloquy that goes on for tens of pages.

These are examples of what fiction writers can get away with when they stretch the normal usage of punctuation and sentence structure. But for most non-fiction writers it's best to stick to the basics and follow the rules – that way, you're less likely to get yourself into grammatical trouble.

Long and run-on sentences

A sentence that's too long is just as problematic as one that's incomplete. Legal documents tend to include long sentences frequently interrupted with qualifications and parentheses, like this:

> This policy applies to all employees, present and prospective, whose total annual remuneration package, consisting of fixed remuneration, guaranteed or target and any other bonuses (including those based on formulas for profit or revenue sharing), the annual present fair value of long-term incentive awards and other long-term awards (excluding buyouts), non-standard relocation/mobility benefits, pension arrangements and any other payments made as part of the remuneration package, is expected to equal or exceed an amount specified from time to time, this amount currently being R5 million.

We forgive you if you didn't bother reading to the end of that sentence ... or, more likely, if you got lost halfway through and gave up. Although it's not grammatically incorrect, that sentence is unreadable (in the sense that it's not designed to be read). It's simply too long and detailed. It's like a shipping container: good for storing things but not so great for living in, unless you thoroughly renovate it.

A particular kind of long sentence to avoid is the run-on sentence, which is when two or more complete sentences are not joined correctly. Run-on sentences look sloppy and are hard to follow. There are various ways to fix them. If you're not sure whether to use a comma or a full stop, play it safe and use a full stop.

RUN-ON SENTENCE	HOW TO FIX IT	REVISED
The public-works programme is expanding, it will reach five million participants by 2025.	*Split into two sentences*	The public-works programme is expanding. It will reach five million participants by 2025.
	Join with "and"	The public-works programme is expanding and will reach five million participants by 2025.
	Rephrase	The expanding public-works programme will reach five million participants by 2025.

If you feel a sentence is too long and needs to be split into parts, look for conjunctions (connecting words such as "and", "or", "but" and "yet") and terms like "for example", "that is", "such as", "in other words" and "which". These words introduce a second level to the sentence in the form of an explanation, qualification, elaboration or example.

This sentence is grammatically complete, but could pose a challenge to the reader:

> In what is being touted by the CEO as a key cash-saving measure at a time when Cricket South Africa are haemorrhaging money (revised loss expectations of some R350 million have been reported for the next four-year period), the board has given the green light for a return to a 12-team model of provincial cricket from the current six-team senior franchise system.

The sentence suffers from two problems. First, the key information is positioned deep in the second half of the sentence. Second, the extra detail in brackets breaks the flow and burdens the reader with detail before they know what the main point is. The second word of the sentence, "what", which is a kind of holding word, indicates that the key point will come later, after some context. But there is too much context, which means that the reader will probably have to reread the sentence to fit all the information together logically so it makes sense.

Improving the sentence could involve splitting it into two and positioning the key point first and the contextual information second:

> The board of Cricket South Africa has given the green light for a return to a 12-team model of provincial cricket from the current six-team senior franchise system. This is being touted by the CEO as a key cash-saving measure at a time when the organisation is haemorrhaging money (revised loss expectations of some R350 million have been reported for the next four-year period).

Framed in this way, the extra detail in brackets is spatially where it belongs – at the very end, available as an optional extra to the reader who'd like to know more.

You might have noticed another small difference between the original and the revised version: "Cricket South Africa are" versus "the organisation is".

Although the organisation is a single entity, it consists of a number of people (bear in mind that in this case we're actually referring to the organisation's board). While it's more grammatically correct to use a singular verb for a singular entity, it's common to use a plural verb too. In a case like this, or when you're referring to a sports team ("Nigeria is playing Kenya this weekend"), we would suggest that the singular is more appropriate. (For more on subject-verb agreement, see the section in Chapter 4 on errors of concord.)

There is often confusion around when to use "that" and when to use "which", and this can lead to problematic longer sentences. The pronouns "that" and "which" help to introduce detail about a noun. They are often used interchangeably but have slightly different functions. "That" serves to define, whereas "which" is non-defining. Some examples:

- Which box has gone missing? (There are many boxes and "which" is used to ask for defining details.)
- The box that contains valuable IT equipment has gone missing. ("That" introduces defining detail about the missing box.)
- The washing machine, which weighs a ton, is broken. (Here, there is one washing machine and "which" introduces an incidental detail about it.)
- The store is out of stock of the washing machine that I want to buy. (There are many washing machines but "that" specifies the desired one.)

When you use "which", ensure it refers to the right item in the sentence. "Which" usually points to the term in the clause or phrase immediately preceding it, and it usually takes a comma to show that it introduces extra information. The following example illustrates how the careless use of "which" can lead to confusion.

RUN-ON SENTENCE WITH "WHICH"	REVISED
These operational challenges and non-capital interventions are currently not explicitly targeted by the corporate plan, **which,** if not done, may continue to undermine operations and hamper efforts to attract additional customers and grow volumes.	These operational challenges and non-capital interventions are currently not explicitly targeted by the corporate plan. If they are not addressed, they may continue to undermine operations and hamper efforts to attract customers and grow volumes.

In the sentence on the left, the reader is left guessing whether "which" is referring to the corporate plan or the operational challenges and non-capital interventions. In the revised version, "they" makes it clear that the second sentence is elaborating on the challenges and interventions, not the corporate plan. A similar problem occurs in the following example, where it's hard to know if "however" is qualifying the first or second part of the sentence.

RUN-ON SENTENCE WITH "HOWEVER"	REVISED
The retail sector has traditionally outperformed the office and industrial sectors**, however,** low economic growth, weak consumer confidence and high unemployment have negatively affected this year's results.	The retail sector has traditionally outperformed the office and industrial sectors. However, low economic growth, weak consumer confidence and high unemployment have negatively affected this year's results.

Beware the kind of run-on sentence that results when you write the way you speak:

> The Minister of Finance spoke to the Minister of Sport, **he said** the programme would be funded in 2023.

If this sentence occurred in a conversation, it might be clear which minister is being referred to as "he" – given that when we are speaking we understand a lot more about context without it needing to be spelt out. But in writing you need to cover your bases and leave no room for confusion:

> The Minister of Finance told the Minister of Sport that the programme would be funded in 2023.

Finally, a point about rhythm. The following comment about E.L. James's publishing sensation *Fifty Shades of Grey* (2011) is not a run-on sentence. But it's a good example of awkward rhythm despite correct grammar. The problem is that the placement of "even" makes the sentence difficult to read:

> *Fifty Shades* even, and the subsequent ubiquity of kink on morning television and in women's magazines, had an impact on people who hadn't read the books.[35]

As a conceptual unit, the incomplete phrase "*Fifty Shades* even" is not easy for our brains to process. It's easier for the reader to hold in mind the unit "*Fifty Shades*". Shifting "even" to after the subclause solves the problem:

> *Fifty Shades*, and the subsequent ubiquity of kink on morning television and in women's magazines, even had an impact on people who hadn't read the books.

Compared with matters of grammar, rhythm is sometimes considered a grey area (as it were) of secondary importance. (For more on rhythm, see Chapter 5.) Let your ear be the judge: is a given sentence easy to read and understand? If you need to use a subclause in your sentence, position it so that it doesn't interrupt the flow too abruptly. It's as important for a sentence to flow comfortably as it is for it to make grammatical sense.

9. Get your word order right

Ambiguity – multiple meanings within a sentence – can be a great source of humour. Consider this remark by Groucho Marx: "Outside of a dog, a book is man's best friend. Inside of a dog, it's too dark to read." This sentence is grammatically correct, but it plays with two possible meanings.

Ambiguity often creeps into a sentence through careless word choice and clumsy sentence construction. This leaves the reader uncertain about which meaning is intended. Take this example:

> The food charity rented a building that in the past had been a nightclub with funding from the Department of Social Development.

Now, it's unlikely the Department of Social Development would provide funding for a nightclub, but the word order in that sentence does suggest that that's the case. After all, "social development" is open to interpretation ...

---

35 Sian Cain, "150m Shades of Grey: How the decade's runaway bestseller changed our sex lives", *The Guardian*, 15 January 2020.

Luckily, in this case we can use common sense to decipher the correct, intended set of relationships. To remove the ambiguity, along with the implication of shadowy dealings on the part of this government department, we need to shift the word order:

> With funding from the Department of Social Development, the food charity rented a building that in the past had been a nightclub.

In some sentences, the word order presents a situation that simply doesn't make sense. The ambiguity in such cases is easy to spot but it's still confusing, as evident in this sentence:

> I will send you the feedback that we discussed later today.

Clearly it's not possible to have had a discussion that will happen later today. Correcting this glitch requires slotting "later today" in at the start of the sentence:

> Later today, I will send you the feedback that we discussed.

To guard against ambiguity, a good rule of thumb is to position the subject of the sentence near the verb and the verb near the object. In the examples below, the sentences on the left would be clearer if the words in bold were placed alongside each other, as shown on the right.

AWKWARD WORD ORDER	REVISED
She spoiled **her presentation** by standing with her back to her audience **on higher education.**	She spoiled her presentation on higher education by standing with her back to her audience.
I have **discussed** the possibility of using renewable energy in the office **with my boss.**	I have discussed with my boss the possibility of using renewable energy in the office.
Customers now have the convenience of an experienced banker **wherever they are** and will be able to communicate via email and telephone.	Wherever they are, customers now have the convenience of being able to communicate via email and telephone with an experienced banker.

Make sure it's clear which subject in a sentence is responsible for an action. This sentence –

> Kenyan prosperity depends on **its** ability to participate in the growing global economy.

is very close to correct, except that the focus is on *prosperity*, not Kenya. A tweak is required:

> Kenyan prosperity depends on the country's ability to participate in the growing global economy.

The positioning and order of words can make all the difference to the meaning of a sentence.

10. Put the main idea up front

Lead with the main idea rather than burying it at the end of the sentence or paragraph. This is particularly important for long, detailed sentences like this one:

> If inflation expectations are not anchored and if currency depreciation is significant and prolonged, an exchange rate-induced price spiral could occur.

If this and if that, then ...: with simpler sentences, this structure won't get you into difficulty. For example: "If you're in the mood on Saturday and the weather is good, we should go to the beach." But where big words and detail are involved, it's best to make your sentence as reader-friendly as possible by starting with the main idea:

> An exchange rate-induced price spiral could occur if inflation expectations are not anchored and if currency depreciation is significant and prolonged.

The same principle applies to the following examples, where one has to read to the end of the sentence to discover the focal action. It doesn't help that both sentences on the left are in the passive voice.

PASSIVE VOICE	ACTIVE VOICE
Because of the anti-oxidants they contain, a diet rich in green leafy vegetables is **recommended by doctors.**	Doctors recommend a diet rich in green leafy vegetables because they contain anti-oxidants.
Transitioning to a consolidated arrangement that locates all debt-management functions within a single unit in the finance ministry **has met with some resistance by stakeholders.**	Stakeholders have resisted consolidating all debt-management functions in a single unit in the finance ministry.

In a sentence with two or more verbs, start with the key verb. In the following example, the two verbs are "migrate" and "estimate", but "estimate" is the key verb. Placing it at the start of the sentence makes it easier to identify the sentence's focus.

KEY VERB AT THE END	LEAD WITH THE KEY VERB
The number of people migrating in search of better socio-economic opportunities **is difficult to estimate.**	It is difficult to estimate the number of people migrating in search of better socio-economic opportunities.

It's often best to position details of time and place at the start of a sentence because they provide a useful frame of reference for the reader. Stating them up front gets them out of the way, preventing confusion that may result when they bring up the rear.

ACTION AND TIME AT END	ACTION AND TIME UP FRONT
In response to investor needs and a broader industry trend away from small bespoke funds to broader asset allocation funds, **we announced plans to simplify our fund offering towards the end of 2019.**	Towards the end of 2019, we announced plans to simplify our fund offering in response to investor needs and an industry trend away from small bespoke funds to broader asset allocation funds.

This principle also applies to organising the content of a document. Opening with an overview helps orientate the reader with useful context. This is particularly important if your text contains a lot of detail. As the authors of the US Securities Exchange Commission's *Plain English Handbook* observe:

> It's hard to absorb the details if you don't know why they are being given to you. Imagine trying to put together a complicated jigsaw puzzle without first seeing the picture of the completed puzzle. An individual piece of information means more to your readers if they know how it fits into the big picture.[36]

So, use the opening paragraph of a piece to frame what follows. In a longer report, this framing section could take the form of a freestanding executive summary (see Chapter 6 for more on summaries).

To wrap up

The principles of clear writing covered in this chapter mainly relate to words, phrases and sentences. Some – like putting the main idea up front – can be usefully applied to a larger block of text, such as a paragraph or section, if not the whole of your piece. As noted earlier, these principles are guidelines to steer by, not strict injunctions to obey. If your line of work requires, for instance, the predominant use of the passive voice, then we hope you can now use it with a better understanding of why it's preferred in certain situations and professions. Our priority is to raise your awareness about the possibilities available to you in every sentence.

Using these principles as a foundation, the next chapter discusses how to organise ideas logically and give them emphasis, making your writing engaging and persuasive.

---

36 Office of Investor Education and Assistance, *A Plain English Handbook*, p. 15.

CHAPTER 3

Making your writing persuasive and easy to read

What makes writing persuasive? Why do some pieces of writing feel effortless to read? Why do others make you feel like you're slogging through a swamp?

In thinking about what makes writing persuasive, it's useful to pose the question in a different form: Why do some people sound unconvincing when they talk? It's likely to be for one or more of the following reasons:

- They ramble and don't seem to know what they're talking about.
- They state the obvious.
- They insist their opinion, feeling or intuition is fact.
- They exaggerate.
- They use inexact language.
- They say things that are factually incorrect.
- They present an illogical argument, and fail to provide good reasons for their assertions.
- They repeat things they heard somewhere – but can't tell you where.
- They care more about the sound of their own voice than whether you understand what they're saying.

By contrast, someone who is persuasive cares about accuracy, brevity and convincing you of their point through precise language and logical argument.

In this chapter, we're going to look more closely at how you can make your writing engaging, persuasive and easy to read. Before we dive into the detail, let's discuss a common difficulty: beginning.

Getting started

Writer's block is one thing, but many of us struggle to get our writing out of the blocks in the first place. Getting started is often the hardest part of writing.

You've done your research, spoken to people, jotted down some ideas. You have a broad sense of what you want to say and a fair amount of information at your disposal. Now, how do you organise it?

You can start by listing your ideas in bullet points. This will give you an overview of the range of information available to you, making it easier to group ideas by topic, identify gaps and leave out irrelevant detail. Once you've shortlisted some workable topics, focus on refining the key points you want to make about each one.

The next step is to sequence the topics logically, given the broader context. What is your starting point? Are you sharing new information? Do you need to argue for or against a claim? Are you presenting a new piece of evidence? Are you suggesting that an assumption needs to be revised? Do you know what your conclusion or key message is?

It's difficult to draft an argument before you start writing, and it might only emerge in the process of organising your information. It sometimes helps to jot down a single sentence that captures the essence of your discussion – or what you think will be the essence. If you're struggling, imagine a friend who doesn't have time to read your piece asks you what it's about. You should be able to tell them the main points in simple terms. This brief summary can be your working storyline that you can refine as you go.

Consider your audience

When you stand up to give a speech at a formal event, you would be wise to read the room. Similarly, as we saw in Chapter 1, it's important to think carefully about your reader before you start writing:

- Who are you writing for?
- What is your relationship to them?
- What is the purpose of your piece?
- What will your audience likely already know about the subject?
- What questions might they ask?

The content you produce should be meaningful to your reader. Don't waste their time with irrelevant detail. Equally, don't assume your reader knows too much – even knowledgeable audiences appreciate simple and succinct writing. Provide enough relevant contextual information so that someone who isn't a specialist in the field can understand what your piece is about. Anticipate questions your reader might ask and weave your responses into the fabric of your piece.

Putting yourself in your reader's shoes holds for other kinds of communication too. For example, podcasts. If you're targeting listeners based in Johannesburg and know that the average commuting time is 30 minutes, don't create a one-hour podcast. In any event, a 30-minute podcast is more likely to hold your listener's attention; it will also force you to edit your content for focused presentation.

Working to limitations can be a great way to stimulate creativity. When you're given 300 words for a newspaper column or 20 PowerPoint slides with 20 seconds to talk about each one (as in PechaKucha presentations), you are forced to write or speak to the point. This is difficult – just as it's difficult to write under pressure – but your reader will appreciate the result. And since writing is meant to be read, it's the reader's judgement that counts.

Get your tone right

The tone you use depends on the kind of writing you're producing and who you're writing for. Your purpose will vary: you may want to inform, motivate, reassure, challenge, apologise, celebrate or show appreciation. Don't talk *at* or *down to* people. Instead, aim to engage *with* them in a way that is open and respectful. To achieve this, you need to use words that resonate with your audience.

WHAT IS TONE?

Tone is your attitude towards a particular audience on a particular occasion. It's conveyed in the words you choose (formal versus conversational), your syntax (the way those words come together), the length of your sentences and whether you use or avoid personal pronouns (like "I", "we" and "our") and contractions ("isn't" versus "is not").

A **conversational tone** is appropriate if you want to address someone in a friendly way. Below is an example of a marketing message from the website of an insurance company. Notice the engaging use of "you", the contractions, the direct sentences, the words like "awesome" and the exclamation mark showing enthusiasm:

> We'll go out of our way to give you an awesome home insurance deal that comes with a few extra benefits too. Like 10% of your premiums back after three claim-free years and a helping hand in a home emergency, any time of the day or night. Whether you're here for buildings cover or contents insurance, we're going to spoil you with a whole bunch of free bonus benefits so that you get the most out of your home insurance!

This approachable tone is notable, even if the concept of "free bonus benefits" for a service that you pay for is egregiously at odds with reality. In any event, you can be conversational while remaining polite and keeping your sentences grammatical. But getting your tone right does involve some careful thought.

Used carelessly, a conversational tone in writing can lead to grammatical sloppiness and overfamiliarity. South African celebrity Bonang Matheba's book *From A to B* (2017) serves as a cautionary tale against neglecting attention to grammar and detail. Written in an engaging tone, the book is wordy, repetitive and strewn with errors. Here's a sample:

> Somizi didn't even realise why I had stopped friends (sic) with him. He thought it was because of something he thinks I think he did, but it was none of that. I stopped being friends with him because he became one of the people who clearly did not have my best interests at heart. It is important to get rid of people who no longer have your best interests at heart, and you don't need to explain yourself, just get out. Just get out and get as far as possible as you can.

Many people who bought the book weren't happy with its poor quality and said so, loudly, on social media.[37] In response, Exclusive Books apologised, removed the book from its shelves and offered a refund to dissatisfied customers. The company's CEO said that he felt Bonang's followers deserved some respect and that it would have been unethical for him to ignore the complaints of readers.

---

37 Refilwe Pitjeng, "Bonang's 'From A to B' book misses writing ABCs", *Eyewitness News*, 3 August 2017.

Don't put yourself in this situation. Be careful not to let your grammar and attention to detail slip when you adopt a less formal tone.

A word on the exclamation mark. Use them sparingly – to exclaim! Or as the Chicago Manual of Style says, to mark "an outcry or an emphatic or ironic comment". Where the exclamation is mild, a full stop will do. When you go down the road of unrestrained exclamation marks, bad things happen! You'll find that you need them more and more!! Really!!!

Overuse of this punctuation mark is rife on social media, where it allegedly signals both friendliness and enthusiasm. This approach has overrun all sorts of correspondence – corporate, commercial, academic – to the point where no email is seen as approachable without the requisite level of grammatically powered bonhomie. Use of the exclamation mark in emails is probably with us to stay. (Thanks!) But outside limited use in that context and in the social media universe, overuse of the exclamation mark is tiresome, and may suggest a certain giddiness on the part of the writer.

Colloquial language is casual language we use when we're talking informally to someone. It usually includes words borrowed from local languages and slang expressions specific to a social group or region: for example, words like "hey", "bro", "cool" and "cheers". This type of language may be suitable for marketing campaigns, where it's used to appeal to a youthful audience. For example, consider this marketing pitch:

> With zero monthly fees and loads of monthly value-adds, MegaU is the ideal bank account for under 19s. Want to take it to the next level? Become moneywise by downloading our feature-packed MegaU App.

A teenager will relate to the choice of words ("loads" and "next level") and sentence structure ("Want to take it to the next level?" instead of "Would you like to access more features?"). Here, the informal tone works. But avoid using this kind of language in conventional business communications. For example, the word "full-blown" sits oddly in the following sentence:

> The anti-smoking awareness campaign has become a full-blown health programme the communities in the area depend on.

Although you could say that "full-blown" is a witty choice for a sentence about smoking, the word jars because it's too informal. A better option would be "comprehensive".

If you choose to use colloquial language, beware of expressions that mean one thing in your region and another somewhere else. For instance, in Johannesburg you might indicate you're going to help someone by saying "I'll sort you out". But if you use this phrase in, say, New York, your listener might think you're threatening them with physical violence. "Just now" is another expression that means different things to different people. To someone from the United States, it means immediately, whereas to a South African it means "after a while", which may be in a few minutes or in an hour.

When we speak, many of us say "try and" when what we mean is "try to", as in "I will try to get it done today". We slip into this habit because it requires a bit more effort to enunciate the words "try to" ("try and" rolls off the tongue more easily). But grammatically, "try and" doesn't make sense in the above sentence. The "and" has the effect of separating the two verbs "try" and "get", so that "I will" seems to apply to them separately: "I will try" and "I will get it done today". This makes it seem like we're intending to do two things rather than one, which is obviously not the case. When you're writing, be alert to grammatical slips like this that we carry over from our habits of speech.

To achieve a **formal tone**, it's best to avoid contractions such as "isn't" and "wasn't". Below is a list of words that are similar in meaning but differ in tone.

LESS FORMAL	MORE FORMAL
ask	request
get	acquire
choose	select
end	conclude
tell	inform
take part in	participate in
make sure	ensure

Here, it's not a matter of "less formal is good" and "more formal is bad", or vice versa. Context should guide your choice of whether to use the less or more formal term. For example, you're likely to use less formal language if you're writing an email to a colleague who you know, but more formal language if you're writing to a client. In a formal report, you would want to avoid using a conversational turn of phrase like "Motorists **do their own thing** when it comes to traffic circles". A better version would be "Motorists <u>tend to disregard</u> road markings around traffic circles".

When you're trying to strike a formal tone, a common mistake is to lapse into professional jargon (professionalese). While it's true that formal expressions tend to be longer than informal ones, the challenge is to keep your tone formal *and* your language clear and concrete, without sounding pompous.

Below are fancy-sounding but abstract sentences on the left, contrasted with more direct, concrete versions on the right. The crucial point here is that the versions on the right *are not informal*. They simply use concrete language that is easier to understand.

ABSTRACT PROFESSIONALESE	CONCRETE ALTERNATIVE
Adverse conditions prevailed throughout the game.	The entire game was played in rain and wind.
The community dialogue intervention will enhance the capability of beneficiaries to optimally manage their bovine assets.	The workshop will teach people in the community how to better manage their cattle.
Members of the workforce will undertake a 360-degree questionnaire assessment to unlock added value in the organisation's culture.	Employees will complete a survey to identify changes they would like to see in the organisation's culture.

As with formatting style (which we'll discuss later in this chapter), so with tone: be consistent within a given piece of writing. There might be one or two words that are out of place, and that's where it's helpful to ask a friend or colleague to look over your work to check that it strikes the right tone throughout.

Write to the point

A good joke should get to the point sooner rather than later. This is also true for writing. Kurt Vonnegut's advice for writers is relevant here: "Use the time of a total stranger in such a way that he or she will not feel the time has been wasted."[38]

Compare the following two sentences:

> Viewed in terms of macroeconomic indicators and fiscal pressures flowing from the recession that began affecting economies at a global level in 2008, South Africa has been affected, and is still affected, by a difficult economic environment.
>
> South Africa is still feeling the effects of the 2008 global financial crisis.

Sentence 1 is likely to lose readers immediately. Sentence 2 cuts to the heart of the matter and provides a stronger foundation to build on. It's not necessary to mention macroeconomic indicators and fiscal pressures to make the point that the economy is struggling. Yes, you might want to elaborate on these technical details, but don't open with them.

Writing to the point is vital for making your writing relevant and engaging. Few readers have the time or patience to wade through paragraphs and pages before getting to the focal point of your piece. It usually takes some drafting to carve out the main point; then you need to position it well to the fore so the reader has a clear view of what's to come.

Below are the first few paragraphs from two articles on "eco-anxiety" – anxiety about climate change, which is widespread in society today. Which piece do you think gets to the point quicker?

Example 1

> Ecology is the study of interactions between organisms and their surroundings in the Earth's biosphere. Climate is an integral part of ecology. It is a summation of atmospheric elements and their variations over a longer period of time; weather is its shorter counterpart.

---

38 Kurt Vonnegut, "8 rules for writing", quoted on the website of the Gotham Writers Workshop from the preface to Vonnegut's short story collection *Bagombo Snuff Box*.

To quote Greek philosopher Heraclitus, "change is the only constant" can be applied to the climate condition these days. As climate patterns change, living beings must work to adapt to those changes.

Charles Darwin introduced the concept of "natural selection" or "survival of the fittest" in his seminal work *On the Origin of Species,* which suggests that those creatures that adapt to the changes in their surroundings have a better chance of surviving as a species.

But the extent to which the climate trends and patterns are changing is verging on beyond adaptability. Climate change has had a negative impact on living creatures, particularly the most conscious species: human beings.

Climate change is an etiology – a cause or a set of causes – for an emerging type of psychological distress that has been termed "eco-anxiety": persistent anxiousness and stress over ecological disasters and environmental threats.[39]

Example 2

Under the bright white lights of a central London exhibition space, a few dozen people are sorting themselves into groups. An instructor tells those that feel extremely worried about climate change to go to the far end of the room. Those that are less worried should stay closer to her. Moments later, she is mostly alone. Thirty feet away, strangers awkwardly cram together, signaling that they suffer "eco-anxiety".

This workshop, organized by King's College London, is one of several events organized in the British capital this fall to help people work through the feelings of anxiety, depression and grief that arise from confronting the fact that, according to the U.N., we now have less than 11 years to prevent catastrophic climate change. "I try not to be hard on myself, because I know I'm doing as much as I can," says Leyla Kaya, a 29-year-old IT consultant. She is vegan, avoids flights and has reduced her non-recyclable waste to less than a liter a month, but she's worried

---

39 Rishita Chandra, "Eco-anxiety: Managing mental health amid climate change impacts", *The Jakarta Post,* 3 December 2019.

by how little action governments and other individuals are taking. "It's really scary. It does get me down."[40]

The author in example 1 takes a far more circuitous route into her topic than the author in example 2. In example 1, the reader is introduced to several different ideas across five paragraphs before being presented with the main topic of discussion.

The author of example 2 takes a more direct approach, hooking the reader's attention immediately by describing a scene in which something happens.

Writing to the point is not just about being concise: it's also about arranging your material so the reader can easily pick up your most important points. Later in this chapter we discuss how to make your key points accessible; but first let's consider the art of developing them into a strong argument.

Build a convincing argument

What is an argument and why do you need one?

If you want a reader to take your writing seriously, you need to build an argument. By "argument" we don't necessarily mean a debate in which you express a strong opinion on a subject or develop a case for or against something, as you might do in an essay or opinion piece. Rather, we use the term in a more general sense to mean giving your ideas coherence by structuring them logically, explaining them, illustrating them with examples and reinforcing them with evidence.

Building an argument involves presenting a core point or key message by moving from a premise, through a set of supporting points, to a conclusion. An argument, in this sense, is similar to a narrative thread that allows the reader to follow the stages of your discussion so that by the time they get to the end they understand how your ideas link together, and why they are valid and worth taking seriously.

An argument needs to have an introduction, a body and a conclusion. In the *introduction* you present your starting point by indicating the topic: What is the issue, challenge or question you are addressing? What event or development has

40 Ciara Nugent, "Terrified of climate change? You might have eco-anxiety", *Time*, 21 November 2019.

prompted the piece? What existing work, interpretation or position are you responding to? If you're presenting a point of view on a subject, what is the context and why should a reader pay attention? The introduction is where you outline your core point or message (expanding on the title of the piece). Avoid providing too much detail in your opening section, because the purpose here is to sketch the context, indicate what is at stake and entice your reader to read on.

The *body* of your argument is where you support your ideas, providing background, context, explanation, reasons, examples and other relevant information to back up and illustrate the claims you make. This is where you dive into the detail. For your argument to be convincing, the detail must be relevant, the evidence credible and your discussion meaningful. An argument has to be carefully built from supporting evidence: it's no good dumping information in the body without arranging it logically, engaging with it closely and showing how it relates to your core point.

The *conclusion* wraps up your argument. Depending on the length and purpose of your piece, the conclusion could contain a key message, main findings, recommendations or reflections on points you made earlier. Avoid ending abruptly or introducing new information in your conclusion: this is where you should provide your reader with a parting shot on the topic, a key takeaway.

Drafting an argument

Ideally, before you start drafting, you should have a good sense of your core idea or message. Don't worry if your message seems unclear; it will gain greater definition in the drafting process. The next step is to settle on a set of supporting points: three to five should be sufficient. From there, you can build your discussion either by adding sub-points or slotting in evidence and examples. It's useful to sketch out your main ideas so you have a rough mind map of the ground you intend to cover. As you draft your discussion in full sentences, keep adjusting this map of key points and checking that they all tie in with your core message – or it may end up that you adjust the core message itself.

A basic approach to drafting an argument is to divide up your document into sections: introduction, body, conclusion. You can then subdivide your body into a series of paragraphs addressing your main supporting points. It may help to give these paragraphs a working subheading to remind you of their focus as you write; you can remove most of these subheadings later if you like. Drafting an argument is rarely a linear process. More often, you add material around different points as thoughts occur to you, making links and filling gaps as your argument takes shape.

Once you have a first draft, test the logical flow of your discussion by labelling each paragraph (just for your own reference) in terms of how it fits into your argument (see discussion below and table on facing page). Ask yourself if your introduction adequately outlines the topic: if it doesn't, refine it until it does. Take the same approach with the other components. A good way to check logical flow is to map your argument by making a list of the topics of each paragraph. It also helps to check that the first words of each paragraph signpost the logical flow of your discussion. The opening phrase of a paragraph is a good place to use logical connectors, which are words that show relationships between ideas (more on this shortly).

To illustrate this quick test of logical flow, we used an article by South African president Cyril Ramaphosa published on the *Financial Times* website.[41] The article's title is "Global response is needed to prevent a debt crisis in Africa". The strapline, which provides more detail, reads "There are several obstacles to the region taking advantage of the G20 debt relief initiative." Arguing that G20 countries need to take urgent measures to prevent a sovereign debt crisis in Africa, the writer discusses four key steps and some obstacles. The table that follows maps the article's argument structure by paragraph, component and opening phrase. Notice how the opening phrases cue the next logical step in the discussion.

41 Cyril Ramaphosa, "Global response is needed to prevent a debt crisis in Africa", *Financial Times*, 30 November 2020. Full text available at https://www.ft.com/content/5f428a4d-bd29-44e6-a307-c97b3f325d7b.

PARAGRAPH	ARGUMENT COMPONENT	OPENING WORD OR PHRASE
1	Introduction	The G20 summit ended last weekend ...
2	Background context	In the early 2000s
3	Background context	Indeed ... several steps ...
4	Step 1	The first ...
5	Obstacles	Unfortunately ...
6	Obstacles	Furthermore ...
7	Step 2	The second step ...
8	Step 3	The third step ...
9	Step 4	Lastly ...
10	Conclusion	For three decades ...

This tabulation shows that there is a clear logical progression to the argument, which makes it easy for a reader to follow the author's ideas. Of course, a strong argument requires more than an elegant structure; it needs solid content: sound reasoning, relevant detail and credible evidence (more on this in a moment). Equally, your content needs to be clearly and logically organised to be persuasive.

Provide good reasons

Consider these statements:

1. She is not a good actress because she doesn't act very well.
2. My friend's son wears glasses so he must be a big reader.
3. It is widely accepted that corporal punishment is good because it teaches children that there are consequences to bad behaviour. I experienced it and I turned out OK.

None of these statements is convincing. The first is an example of circular reasoning (*since X, therefore X*): the claim is not supported with evidence but simply repeated in different words. The second draws a conclusion based on insufficient evidence. The third is problematic because it generalises without evidence ("It is widely accepted": By whom? When? Where?), lacks definition of an assumption (What is meant by "good"? For whom is it "good"?), does not qualify itself by noting alternative points of view or other ways of achieving the same result, and presents the speaker's assessment of herself as singular proof. These are some of the common pitfalls in building an argument.

For an argument to be convincing, there has to be a progression from a premise, through acceptable, sufficient, relevant reasons and evidence, to a conclusion. Without these ingredients, your claims risk remaining in the realm of opinion, speculation, generalisation and irrelevance – easy to dismiss. Below, we look more closely at some ways you can strengthen your argument.

Does the following example present a compelling argument against the banning of guns?

> It's a cliché, but it's true: Guns don't kill people, people kill people. Firearms are a tool, and they can be used for good or ill. It's certainly the case the guns can be used to commit robberies, murder, and terrorism. However, there are also legitimate uses for guns, including sports, hunting, hobbyist collecting, and personal protection. Getting rid of a particular tool will not stop people committing acts of violence. Instead, we need to address the root causes that drive people to perpetrate violence, including looking seriously at whether the mental health system is performing as it should.
>
> We do not ban tools just because they are dangerous. Tens of thousands of Europeans die in car accidents ever year, yet we don't ban cars. Terrorists have used cars and trucks to commit atrocities, yet (again) we don't ban cars and trucks. Indeed, terrorists in Europe have resorted to using knives and cars precisely because guns are so well-regulated across the European Union. So, banning guns does not stop violence.[42]

Not really. The opening statement is weak for two reasons. One, it starts with the wishy-washy "It's a cliché, but it's true", which tells us nothing. And two, it creates a false binary between people and guns (as if it's either the one or the other that kills people). The comparison of guns to other kinds of tools is misleading as

42 Debating Europe, "Arguments for and against banning guns".

guns are designed to cause harm whereas most tools (even dangerous ones) are not. The claims are not supported by convincing, fact-based evidence.

In contrast, consider this example, which is an extract from an article on why independent, fact-based journalism is good for democracy and should receive public funding.

> Local journalism is failing in the United States. Many of us learn in school that a free society requires a free press, but we rarely reflect on what it actually means to lose the fourth estate. Democracies need independent, fact-based journalism to provide a voice for a diverse range of people, to watchdog the powerful, and to keep members of a society informed. Study after study has found that without access to local news, people are less civically engaged and less likely to vote. The demise of local newspapers – which are still by far the main source of original reporting in their communities – is also linked to a rise in local corruption and an increase in polarization, as news consumers rely more on partisan-inflected national outlets for their information.
>
> This crisis arose because the news media's commercial imperatives never fully aligned with democratic objectives. The market simply can't support the levels of journalism – especially local, but also international, policy, and investigative reporting – that a healthy democracy requires. Arguably, this has always been the case, but it's especially true today, as newspapers are hollowed out or closed down across the country, leaving vast news deserts in their wake. All of us who wish for a democratic future – including the business community – have a stake in ensuring that local news media survives. We must come together to build a media ecosystem that treats journalism as an essential public service.[43]

The article opens with a simple declarative statement. This is followed by an explanation of why accurate local journalism is vital (it supports democracy by ensuring diverse perspectives are represented) and the adverse consequences of its absence (a rise in corruption and polarisation). Each claim is backed with a link to a source (hyperlinks are underlined). The second paragraph explains

43 Victor Pickard, "Journalism's market failure is a crisis for democracy", *Harvard Business Review*, 12 March 2020.

how the news media depends on market forces, which are not democratic. These two paragraphs provide a foundation for the argument in the final sentence that journalism should be seen as an essential public service.

Reinforce your points with evidence

A point is more persuasive when supported with evidence. A good rule of thumb is to provide one piece of evidence for each point that requires it. There are many kinds of evidence: facts, statistics, data represented in graphs and tables, quotations from interviews and written sources. Beware of overquoting or overreferencing. An argument doesn't automatically emerge from a patchwork of quotations. You need to use them thoughtfully to form an argument where you assert your idea, discuss it, analyse it, provide evidence to back up the assertion and end with concluding remarks. If you quote or reference too often, you risk not leaving enough room for your own voice to come through clearly.

Reference appropriately

Ensure that the information and anecdotes you use are relevant. Strong evidence is obtained from a reliable source that is widely corroborated and detailed. Acknowledge possible shortcomings. Depending on what you're writing, you may need to provide references for the evidence you include. For example, if you quote someone's words, note who spoke them, when and in what context. This allows an interested reader to consult your sources. Clear referencing that adheres to a particular citation style is a sign of intellectual honesty and positions your work in dialogue with that of others.

When you're referencing, beware of plagiarising another person's work – in other words, taking someone else's words *or even their ideas* and passing them off as your own. Plagiarism is a serious intellectual offence, particularly in academic writing. Academic research depends on citing the work of other academics, so be sure to provide the relevant information about the evidence you use. If you're a student, ask your lecturer to recommend the most appropriate referencing convention for your subject (such as Harvard, MLA or Chicago).

Avoid stating the obvious

Unless you're going to make an interesting point about something that everyone knows, avoid stating the obvious. Here's an example of what not to do:

> Reading the Afterword subsequent to finishing the novel is as important as reading the Foreword prior to starting it, as this helps put things into perspective about the nature and content of the novel.

Given that a foreword and an afterword by definition precede and follow a text, we are not learning anything new here.

Avoid making generalised claims from small studies. It's important to provide a balanced assessment of a topic. If you're writing for the media, get corroborating evidence for your observations from different sources. If you're discussing the views of one party in a dispute, give other involved parties the opportunity to respond. Strive to be balanced – presenting facts, not just opinions.

In the current era, we've witnessed a proliferation of disinformation and misinformation, facilitated by the internet and amplified by social media. This is information that is false or misleading, and based on little, unreliable, invalid or no evidence (disinformation is conveyed with the intention to deceive whereas misinformation may be conveyed mistakenly). To give your writing credibility, it's imperative to use reputable sources and to verify the information you reproduce in your work. Beware of simply quoting a finding from the most recent study that makes news headlines, as there is often context that complicates or qualifies that finding. Moreover, new and alternative views are sure to emerge in due course. As the writer, your role is not just to aggregate information but to explain it in a way that makes it intelligible and relevant to your reader. This critical attitude should inform the way you read as much as the way you write ... and hopefully it will rub off on your readers too.

Use "I" when appropriate

There's no firm rule for when to use "I" – the "first person" – to argue a point. It could be appropriate in an opinion piece, where you're writing as an expert or with special knowledge of a subject. But using "I" is not an excuse to present a poorly reasoned argument. In a blog post, "I" or "we" is a good way of personalising your writing, making it more approachable. In an essay or report, it's generally more appropriate to present your points impersonally. A reader should be able to arrive at the same conclusions on the basis of your logic and evidence.

Students are often advised to avoid using the first person in an academic essay because it foregrounds your point as an opinion – which means that it is not necessarily backed by evidence. But often your task in an essay is precisely to present *your* interpretation of a topic. That doesn't mean every sentence should begin with "I". Instead, you need to find a way to present your views so that the reader is convinced by their validity and accuracy.

Below is an example of two approaches to making the same point in an undergraduate essay on Achebe's novel *Things Fall Apart* (Okonkwo is the main character).

A FIRST-PERSON STATEMENT	AN IMPERSONAL STATEMENT
I do not believe that it was the arrival of the missionaries that triggered the destruction of Okonkwo's society. I think it began long before that.	It was not the arrival of the missionaries that triggered the destruction of Okonkwo's society. The decline began long before that.

In the above example, the impersonal statement is a more definite way of stating your view without drawing attention to it as an opinion. Omitting the "I" doesn't reduce the force of the point; on the contrary, it makes the point more persuasive.

It's sometimes difficult to avoid using "I", and trying to do so can result in awkward sentences, particularly in research proposals and reports to funders. In a research or funding proposal, it makes sense to present your plans, intentions and goals in the first person – and that includes writing as "we", provided it's clear to whom "we" refers. If you speak about "the researcher", the reader might assume that the researcher is someone other than the author of the proposal, which would be odd if your name is on the cover page.

Below are contrasting examples of phrasing from a research proposal. To break the monotony of starting every sentence with "I", use the passive voice (as shown in the second sentence in the right-hand column).

AWKWARD IMPERSONAL PHRASING	DIRECT FIRST-PERSON PHRASING
In the study, the researcher intends to design a decision-making tool based on the outcomes of the qualitative study. The intention is for the participating business owners to review the tool before it is implemented. What is most important is for the researcher to develop a tool that can help business owners make better strategic decisions.	In this study, I plan to design a decision-making tool based on the outcomes of the qualitative study. The participating business owners will review the tool before it is implemented. My priority is to develop a tool that can help business owners make better strategic decisions.

While the version in the right-hand column is more direct, the ideas are still clumsily organised. A better solution would be to resequence the ideas more logically, trim unnecessary words and remove the first person so that the focus is on the components of the study, as follows:

> The aim of this study is to develop a tool to help business owners make better strategic decisions. Participating business owners will review the tool before implementing it.

In speech, "I" plays an important role in stamping the speaker's words with charisma and conviction. For more on this, see our discussion of speechwriting in Chapter 6.

Avoid overwriting and overstatement

Overwriting happens when you use too many colourful words and images in a passage. There's no harm in using adjectives or images occasionally to make a point more vivid, but avoid dressing up your writing too much. If the backbone of your piece is an argument, then the persuasiveness of your piece depends on how you argue your points and the evidence you present – not the breadth of your vocabulary or the number of adjectives you can cram into each sentence.

Take this example: "As I rode the motorbike, the wind rushed over my bare head with unrestrained exuberance, flooding every cavity of my ears with a mighty roar." You have a strong verb in "rushed", so there's no need for "unrestrained exuberance" (exuberance, in any case, implies bursting restraints). The verb "flooding" is unnecessary too. How many cavities does a typical human ear have? The answer's not important – because if you've used a strong verb, you don't need to follow it up with another strong verb: "filling my ears" will do fine. Revised, the sentence reads: "As I rode the motorbike, the wind rushed over my bare head and roared in my ears."

In the following passage, the words in bold could be toned down or cut altogether:

> When South Africa emerged from **the stranglehold of** apartheid in 1994, the **newly minted** nation and its liberation leaders were welcomed **with a warm embrace** by the regional and international community. South African business leaders, **barons of Afrikaner and English capital** – once viewed with disdain for exploiting black workers to shore up the apartheid state – were also **eagerly** embraced. South African business did not squander **a minute of** this goodwill as this change of fortune could not have happened **a moment too soon**."

Apartheid is a byword for racist oppression, so there's no need to use "strangle hold" to heighten the drama of the country's emergence into democracy. Similarly, a word like "embrace" implies warmth and willingness, so "warm" and "eagerly" are unnecessary. In the last sentence, you might notice, too, the awkwardness of mentioning "this change of fortune" when "this goodwill" has just been mentioned and following up "a minute of" with "a moment". The overwriting here results in repetition.

Overwriting is to be avoided, but that doesn't mean you should never reach for an adjective or an adverb.

WHAT'S THE DIFFERENCE BETWEEN AN ADJECTIVE AND AN ADVERB?

An adjective describes a noun, for example, "the **large** crowd", while an adverb describes how an action (a verb) is performed, for example, "she laughed **loudly**".

Some well-known writers have strong views on which words you should avoid using, and often the adjective and adverb are attacked as unnecessary.

One of George Orwell's six rules for clear writing is: "If it is possible to cut a word out, always cut it out."[44] In *The Elements of Style*, Strunk and White tell us that

44 George Orwell, "Politics and the English language" (1946).

"Rich, ornate prose is hard to digest, generally unwholesome, and sometimes nauseating."[45] And Stephen King, the accomplished writer of horror fiction, has said, "The road to hell is paved with adverbs."[46] (Incidentally, King is a big fan of Strunk and White, observing approvingly of *The Elements of Style* that "[t]here is little or no detectable bullshit in that book".[47])

There's wisdom in these pronouncements, and they are memorably forceful. But a balanced view is sensible. In his article "Don't ditch the adverb, the emoji of writing", Gary Nunn quotes his former creative writing teacher, the novelist Kate Forsyth, on why adverbs have an important role to play:

> "Adverbs are an essential part of a writer's toolbox," she says. "Used judiciously, they add emotional depth and create clarity. Think of them as emojis: helping the recipient understand the emotional tone. They can also bring rhythm and texture to a sentence. Bare isn't always best." She cites the Emily Dickinson poem: "Because I could not stop for death, he kindly stopped for me." The adverb "kindly," Forsyth says, is "crucial – the whole meaning hangs upon it."[48]

The more experienced you become as a writer, the more you will develop a feel for when an adverb or adjective adds an extra dab of colour or ounce of energy to a sentence – and when it does the opposite. You will also develop a surer sense of where to position the adverb so it modifies the correct word. The difference in the meaning of these two sentences hinges on the position of the adverb "tragically":

> Tragically, the playwright did not live to see his play performed.
>
> The playwright did not live to see his play performed tragically.

In the first sentence, "tragically" applies to the whole statement about the playwright not living to see his play performed, whereas in the second sentence it applies only to the nature of the performance. Keep your eyes peeled for how the meaning of words can shift with their position in a sentence.

---

45 William Strunk, Jr, and E.B. White, *The Elements of Style*, p. 72.

46 Stephen King, *On Writing*, p. 215.

47 Stephen King, *On Writing*, p. 18.

48 Gary Nunn, "Don't ditch the adverb, the emoji of writing", *The Guardian*, 29 April 2019.

Like overwriting, **overstatement** – puffing up the importance of your points – does no good. Here's an example: "Successful investing depends on the deep insights of specialists." Don't overegg the pudding. One would expect a specialist to have special insights, and an insight by definition goes to the heart of a matter.

Another example, this time from a review of a theatre production:

> This musical is epic – large cast, vivid lighting, stunning musical arrangements and knock-out dance sets. The dancing is astounding and groundbreaking for a mainstream musical: edgy and gritty. The voices are breathtaking. We have such remarkable talent in our city! The women in particular are spectacular with nuanced big voices filling the stage. I was blown away by the entire cast.

You might be enthusiastic about your subject, but avoid gushing. Using too many superlatives implies you don't appreciate their value. Here, "astounding", "groundbreaking", "breathtaking", "spectacular" and "blown away" are different ways of saying that you're at a loss for words – and not just because you're so impressed by the production.

MIND YOUR MODIFIERS

Think carefully before using modifiers like "very", "really", "quite" and "rather" to qualify a point. As Strunk and White rather dramatically put it, "[T]hese are the leeches that infest the pond of prose, sucking the blood of words."[49] Similarly, avoid the British habit of qualifying your statements with words like "rather", "quite" and "a bit", unless you really need to be measured or a bit diplomatic.

Ensure logical flow

Start strongly

Below are the opening paragraphs of two articles, both on the "fourth industrial revolution" in Africa. On the basis of these openings, which article would you rather read?

49 William Strunk, Jr, and E.B. White, *The Elements of Style*, p. 73.

Example 1 from "What 4IR means in the context of South Africa"

> From the Internet of things (IoT) to Artificial Intelligence (AI) to smart cities to the Fourth Industrial Revolution (4IR), the list of buzzwords is steadily growing with a shortage of tangible and visible planning on how this will change the lives for the citizens of a low-income country beset by unemployment and poverty and a struggling economy such as South Africa.[50]

Example 2 from "Revolutionary technologies will drive African prosperity – this is why"

> Right now, we're at a tipping point in Africa's development. We're hurtling headlong into the Fourth Industrial Revolution (4IR), which has the potential to turbocharge the socio-economic development of the entire African continent. We've got the youngest continent in the world, with 60% of Africa's 1.25 billion people under the age of 25. If we make the right decisions in the next few years, we could pave a bold new path of African prosperity.[51]

The first example consists of a long sentence packed with ideas and three acronyms, with the focal point (South Africa) positioned at the end. The second example has shorter, punchier sentences. It creates some suspense in the first sentence (what kind of tipping point?), followed by data points, followed by a sentence capturing the article's focus. Example 2 is more likely to appeal to the reader, if only because it seems the author has a firmer grasp of their material.

These two openings reflect how the rest of each article will read: the first is more meandering, the second more focused. Interestingly, this difference is also evident in their titles, with the heading of the second example more likely to engage the reader immediately.

These examples demonstrate the importance of crafting a strong title and opening paragraph. Both should grab the reader's attention and make her want

50 Eckard Zollner, "What 4IR means in the context of South Africa", ICT Opinion South Africa, www.bizcommunity.com, 20 August 2019.

51 Cathy Smith, "Revolutionary technologies will drive African prosperity – this is why", www.weforum.org, 1 September 2019.

to read on. Your opening paragraph, and ideally your title too, should outline the topic and provide enough context to give the reader a clear idea of the focus and significance of your piece. The first few paragraphs are also a good place to pose questions that will be explored later. Those questions need to be specific and interesting enough to propel the reader through the rest of the piece.

WHO, WHAT, WHEN, WHERE ...

Journalists are often told to present the five Ws and an H (who, what, where, when, why and how) in the first paragraph, because the reader of a news article typically wants to know the basic facts of an event before progressing to an interpretation. However, this approach isn't always appropriate in other kinds of writing. In some cases, it makes sense to avoid including too much detail in your opening paragraphs. Make a good first impression by being clear and direct about the question or issue you're addressing, and how and why it matters to the reader.

Think of your introduction as provisional until you've written the bulk of your piece. Once you've completed a first draft, you can go back and refine the introduction. You may want to outline your argument up front and save the clinching insights for the conclusion. In your conclusion, you could reinforce the claim made in the introduction (if there is one), pose a question that needs to be answered, propose a strategy for the future or outline next steps.

Whichever approach you choose, be sure to make your opening and closing paragraphs as strong as possible. A piece that starts flat is unlikely to be read. One that trails off inconsequentially, as if the writer lost interest and left the room, is likely to leave the reader unconvinced.

Paragraph effectively

Like electricity, paragraphs are often taken for granted until they're absent. Consider them an essential service for the reader. They create breathing space in the text, making it easier to read, and help you organise different ideas. There's no rule for how long a paragraph should be, but two to five sentences is generally sufficient. A series of one-sentence paragraphs will make the text feel fragmented.

Paragraph length varies for different publications. Short paragraphs tend to be used in online writing (for example, blogs, news reports and company newsletters), while longer paragraphs are common in documents containing research or analysis (such as academic papers and annual reports). You'll recall that one of the clear writing principles discussed in Chapter 2 was to put the main idea up front, particularly in longer, more detailed sentences. The same applies to paragraphs: inform the reader of the paragraph's topic or focus near the beginning.

Use logical connectors

Sentences need to be linked to form a fluent and coherent passage. To avoid presenting a laundry list of points or statements, use logical connectors.

Below are two examples of weakly linked ideas, and ways to improve them. The first example, about renewable energy, lacks coordinating conjunctions to indicate logical relationships. In the second example, concerning economic policy, the repeated use of "this" doesn't specify what in the previous sentence is being referred to.

WEAK LINKS BETWEEN IDEAS	STRONG LINKS
A reliable supply of electricity is vital to South Africa's development plans. The country has now developed the Integrated Resource Plan (IRP). The current energy mix is dominated by coal and the IRP aims to significantly reduce this source of energy in future. South Africa plans to boost the production of renewable energy, particularly wind and solar. There is also a need for advanced technology to support this infrastructure. So coal remains the backbone of the country's electricity supply.	A reliable supply of electricity is vital to South Africa's development. <u>To ensure adequate and sustainable supply</u>, the country has developed the Integrated Resource Plan (IRP). <u>Although</u> the current energy mix is dominated by coal, the IRP aims to significantly reduce this source of energy in future. South Africa plans to boost the production of renewable energy, particularly wind and solar, <u>but</u> there is a need for advanced technology to support this infrastructure. <u>For now, and in the near future</u>, coal remains the backbone of the country's electricity supply.

Lower international commodity prices are expected to put pressure on Transnet's heavy-haul rail operations for the foreseeable future. **This** is because mineral commodities form a large portion of Transnet's total freight volume. **This,** combined with structural reforms under way in China, the largest export market for many of South Africa's key metal and mineral commodities, will have a significant impact on Transnet. **This** means it is therefore a risk for capital investments to focus on expanding capacity that serves a market that seems to be undergoing fundamental restructuring.	Lower international commodity prices are expected to put pressure on Transnet's heavy-haul rail operations in the near term because mineral commodities form a large portion of Transnet's total freight volume. The effect of weaker commodity prices will be compounded by structural reforms under way in China, the largest export market for many of South Africa's key metals and minerals. Given the restructuring under way in China, capital investments focused exclusively on expanding capacity to serve this market are a significant risk.

Transitional phrases, like those shown in the table below, are an essential part of the writer's toolkit. They create relationships between ideas and help build an argument. Beware: overusing these terms will pad your sentences so they are needlessly wordy, so use them judiciously.

PURPOSE	TRANSITION WORD OR PHRASE
To sequence points	first, second, third, last, finally
To specify time	next, later, meanwhile, subsequently, while
To repeat or sum up	in short, in sum, overall, once again
To indicate an outcome	due to, as a result, consequently
To extend a list	also, further, furthermore, in addition
To qualify a point	but, yet, despite, although, even though, however, nevertheless, nonetheless, moreover
To compare and contrast	similarly, likewise, in contrast, on the contrary
To indicate likelihood	of course, in fact, certainly, likely, probably, surely, after all, as expected
To advance an argument	thus, therefore, for this reason, so, accordingly

Consider the following four passages:

- I walked to the station. It was raining. The train was late. I got wet.
- I walked to the station even though it was raining. I got wet waiting for the train, which was late.
- I walked to the station. Because it was raining, the train was late. I got wet while waiting for it to arrive.
- I walked to the station. A torrential downpour delayed the train and soaked me in the process.

All four are grammatically correct, but there are slight differences in how the information they contain is organised. The first example is staccato: it doesn't flow. The second and third passages have better flow and indicate relationships of cause and effect. The final example adds a bit of flair (assuming that it was a downpour and not a drizzle and that you did get soaked rather than refreshingly dampened).

Make key points accessible

In Chapter 1, when we discussed the qualities that make a document easy to read, we quoted from *A Plain English Handbook*:

> A plain English document uses words economically and at a level the audience can understand. Its sentence structure is tight. Its tone is welcoming and direct. Its design is visually appealing. A plain English document is easy to read and looks like it's meant to be read.

You might have great points, but if you don't present them effectively on the page, they won't have the impact you hope for. Headings, bullet points, bold and italics are useful tools for focusing your reader's attention on the main ideas.

Headings

A heading serves as a signpost for the reader by capturing or reflecting the main idea. And yet it is often treated as an afterthought. This is not surprising given that generally one decides on a heading after writing a section of text. But bear in mind that it's the *first* thing the reader will see and use to orient themselves.

To be effective, a heading needs to be short and specific. The same principle applies to slide headings in presentations and headings for graphs, figures and tables. You may find it's easier to come up with a title and subheadings once you've finished writing your piece.

Avoid repetition between a subheading and the text below it. In the following example, the sentence immediately below the subheading is unnecessary, as are the words "responsible for" in each of the cells under Responsibility.

Roles and responsibilities

Key roles and responsibilities to achieve the policy requirements are set out below.

ROLE	RESPONSIBILITY
Resourcing	Responsible for enforcing adherence to policy requirements
Hiring manager	Responsible for implementing policy requirements
Risk manager	Responsible for performing an independent audit of policy execution

Here's another example of a subheading not being used effectively. It's taken from a human resources policy document.

In scope

This policy applies to:

(a) The company and all its subsidiaries.

(b) All employees and workers of any entity within the paragraph above.

(c) Graduates, learners and interns are in scope.

Yet again, legal language serves up an example of overformality introducing unnecessary complication. Under point (b), the phrase "of any entity within the paragraph above" is excessive given that the previous point is a five-word sentence. Under point (c), there's no need to write "are in scope" – we know this from the section heading.

If you're following a document template, check that all the subheadings are relevant and that you've placed your content beneath the correct heading. You may need to create a new subheading and section to accommodate content that doesn't fit under the existing headings.

Bullet points

If you want to make a series of points at point-blank range, as it were, use bullet points. They're a great way of elevating key points from detailed content. Avoid using them when they're not necessary, or overusing them: a document full of bullet points defeats their purpose.

Bullet points are best used when points can be listed in any order. If the list is sequential (for example, you're listing steps in a process or items in order of importance), then a numbered list is more appropriate.

The table below shows two examples where bullet points are not the best format for presenting the information. In the first example, the first bullet point expands on the opening statement, while the second addresses a slightly different point. In the second example, the points are too short to justify bulleting.

UNNECESSARY BULLET POINTS	REVISED
A national budget is, essentially, an educated guess: • The finance ministry makes assumptions about macroeconomic performance or the effects of new tax and fiscal policies on revenue collection. • Spending agencies adopt these assumptions and make their own about new and old project plans.	A national budget is, essentially, an educated guess. The finance ministry makes assumptions about macroeconomic performance or the effects of new tax and fiscal policies on revenue collection. Spending agencies, in turn, adopt these assumptions in developing their project plans.
Lump-sum investments can be made by any of the following payment methods: • Direct debit. • Electronic transfer.	Lump-sum investments can be made by direct debit or electronic transfer.

Throughout your document, take care to format your lists consistently or in line with the house style (if there is one) of the organisation you're writing for. One approach is to capitalise the first word of each bullet point and place a full stop at the end of each. Alternatively, if the list of bullet points is introduced by a sentence (or sentence fragment), you could leave the first word of each bullet point in lower case and place a full stop at the end of the last point. Using semicolons after bullet points is outdated and unnecessary. The bullet point does the same job as a semicolon: separating items in a list.

It's important to be consistent when using lists. For instance, you might need to ensure that all bullet points are in the active voice or begin with the same kind of verb. The following example shows how inconsistent wording can result in awkwardness.

INCONSISTENT PHRASING	CONSISTENT USE OF VERBS
The workshop will cover: • Understanding the nature of conflict • Manage customers' expectations • How to deal with difficult situations • Repairing relationships with customers.	The workshop will cover: • <u>Understanding</u> the nature of conflict • <u>Managing</u> customers' expectations • <u>Dealing</u> with difficult situations • <u>Repairing</u> relationships with customers.

Make sure your listed points flow logically from the sentence that introduces them.

LACK OF FLOW	REVISED
We would like to keep you updated on developments in the agricultural sector. **You can read the latest news in:** • ***Agrifair*, this is our bimonthly magazine,** which is available to subscribers online and in hard copy. • **Every week we produce an email newsletter,** *AgriHarvest*, featuring sector highlights, market insights and profiles of market leaders. • **We also run a quarterly podcast,** *From Seed to Success*, showcasing interviews with experts on innovative tools and methods.	We would like to keep you updated on developments in the agricultural sector. We share news through three channels: • *Agrifair*, our bimonthly magazine, which is available to subscribers online and in hard copy. • *AgriHarvest*, a weekly email newsletter featuring sector highlights, market insights and profiles of market leaders. • *From Seed to Success*, a quarterly podcast showcasing interviews with experts on innovative tools and methods.

When a bullet point consists of a long sentence or more than one sentence, it may be helpful to put the key words in bold, like this:

Our new approach to human resources has three elements:

- **Centres of Excellence** will set policy, governance and strategy in areas such as recruitment, employee relations, rewards, and learning and development.
- **Employee Services** will consist of centralised functions such as payroll and the e-Services portal.
- **Advisory Services**, which are being established in all departments, will ensure that the human resources agenda is aligned with the needs and challenges of each department.

Italics are generally reserved for the titles of publications like books and newspapers, or to indicate that you're using a non-English word, like *lobola*.

Foreign words that are commonly used in English are written in roman (upright) font – for example: indaba, trek, veld, incognito.

Language is an organic, ever-changing thing. Some words go out of fashion while others are coined and added to our lexicon as the world changes. If you're unsure whether a foreign word should take italics, look it up in a good dictionary (like the Oxford English Dictionary or the Merriam-Webster Dictionary): if it appears there, then it can be written in roman type.

Present your work neatly

You're interviewing someone for a job. The candidate arrives with food stains on his shirt, his shoelaces untied and his hair unbrushed. Would you overlook these details? Probably not.

The same principle applies to your writing. A clean, orderly layout gives readers a positive first impression and allows them to focus on content without being distracted by how it's presented on the page. All too often, written reports resemble a ransom note. A design that increases readability doesn't happen by itself. Putting aside time to check the formatting of your work is a habit of good housekeeping – it's just as important as checking the accuracy and appropriateness of the words themselves. Paying close attention to the following aspects of formatting will enhance the impact of your work.

Font and spacing

Here are some basic points to apply:

- Choose a font that's easy to read, such as Times New Roman, Calibri or Arial.
- Make sure it's big enough to read: 11 or 12 point is the standard size.
- Avoid using font colours that are difficult to read. Black is standard.
- Avoid italicising a whole sentence or passage, as this can be more difficult to read and defeats the purpose of highlighting key words.

Generally, if you're quoting more than three lines of text, set it apart from the rest of your paragraph by leaving a line space before and after it and indenting it on the left and right, like this:

It's easy to ignore the value of space on the page until you're faced with a page crammed with text. Let your words breathe by using adequate and consistent line and paragraph spacing – 1.15-point, 1.5-point or 2-point spacing are all fine.

Spelling

Organisations and institutions usually have a preferred style, outlined in a style guide, that they require you to follow. If they don't have a preference, then decide up front whether you'll be using British or American spelling and be consistent throughout your piece. Most African countries where English is widely spoken use British spelling conventions.

BRITISH SPELLING	US SPELLING
organi**se**, recogni**se**, analy**se**	organi**ze**, recogni**ze**, analy**ze**
col**our**, hon**our**	col**or**, hon**or**
cent**re**	cent**er**
progra**mme**	progra**m**
trave**ll**ed, cance**ll**ed	trave**l**ed, cance**l**ed
defen**c**e, licen**c**e	defen**s**e, licen**s**e

In British and American English, different words are often used to refer to the same thing. In countries where British English dominates, people will refer to petrol, queues, flats and lifts, whereas Americans refer to gas, lines, apartments and elevators. The names of organisations remain the same regardless of spelling convention. So, even if you're using British spelling, you should still refer to the World Trade Cent**er** or the World Health Organi**z**ation. South African English includes words drawn from Dutch, Afrikaans and African languages, such as "kloof", "vlei" and "tsotsi". Some English words have a different meaning in South Africa, for example, "robot" (traffic light) and "café" (corner store).

MAKE SPELLCHECK WORK FOR YOU

In Microsoft Word, remember to set the language for proofing tools such as Spellcheck by navigating to the language settings and selecting the appropriate spelling convention.

If you're not using a style guide, then the best approach to spelling and punctuation is simply to be consistent. Decide, for example, whether you will write "data is" or "data are", "subset" or "sub-set", and stick to your decision throughout your document. Your priority is to ensure that the reader is not distracted by little inconsistencies in style or format. You want their attention to be focused squarely on the content of your writing.

Acronyms

An acronym saves you having to write out a set of terms that are mentioned often in a document. It's designed to conserve energy and space and make a text easier to read. But when used loosely, it can turn a passage into a brambly thicket – *not* the kind of thing a reader wants to get involved with.

An acronym is formed from the initial elements (usually the first letter) of a phrase or a word. For example, "WHO" is the acronym for the World Health Organization. No full stops are needed for acronyms: it's "UN", not "U.N." But when acronyms are overused, they become a form of jargon, turning your writing into alphabet soup.

UNDERSTANDING ABBREVIATIONS AND ACRONYMS

An abbreviation is a way of shortening a longer word or set of words. For example, "Dr" for "doctor", "Prof." for "Professor", "i.e." for "that is" ("id est" in Latin). An acronym is a kind of abbreviation. It contains some of the initial elements of a phrase to form a new word. For example, "SMS" for "short message service" and "AIDS" for acquired immunodeficiency syndrome.

Use the shortened word or phrase only if the term occurs repeatedly in a paragraph or document and the acronym makes the text easier to read. Write the term out in full the first time it's mentioned, followed by the acronym in brackets. Thereafter, use only the acronym. For example, "The United Nations (UN) is an international organisation founded in 1945. It is currently made up of 193 member states. The mission and work of the UN are guided by the purposes and principles contained in its founding charter."

Some things to remember:

- When you write out an acronym in words, the words are only capitalised if they form an official name. For example: equity prices on the Johannesburg Stock Exchange (JSE) increased by 2% in the first quarter.
- Use lower case if the term represented by the acronym is a common noun. So: gross domestic product (GDP).
- Conjunctions such as "and" are generally not included in an acronym: for example, the Research and Early Development (RED) team is based in Cape Town.
- When they are written out, some acronyms take punctuation. For example, the hyphen in non-governmental organisation (NGO) and the apostrophe in Purchasing Managers' Index (PMI).
- Indicate the plural of an acronym with a small "s": FAQs, ATMs.

The examples below contrast incorrect and correct use of acronyms. In the first example, the acronym stands for a common noun, which is written in lower case. In the second example, "Sustainable Development Goals" should be in title case because it's an official name, while "benefit-cost ratio" takes lower case as it's a common noun.

INCORRECT	CORRECT
The project discusses the possibility of developing an **Early Warning System**. An effective **Early Warning System (EWS)** alerts local populations before floods, helping to save lives and prevent damage to infrastructure.	The project discusses the possibility of developing an early warning system (EWS). An effective EWS alerts local populations before floods, helping to save lives and prevent damage to infrastructure.
In its analysis of achieving the **sustainable development goals (SDGs)**, the World Bank estimated that the **Benefit-Cost Ratio (BCR)** of achieving universal access to basic water is 3.3.	In its analysis of achieving the Sustainable Development Goals (SDGs), the World Bank estimated that the benefit-cost ratio (BCR) of achieving universal access to basic water is 3.3.

Some acronyms will be so familiar to your audience that you won't need to write them out in full at first mention. For example, most people will know what an ATM is, so you don't need to spell out automated teller machine. A few acronyms have been used so often that they can now be written as nouns and are pronounced as such (rather than each initial enunciated separately): for example, AIDS.

SEARCH FOR ACRONYMS

To search for acronyms in a document, use the "Find" function in Microsoft Word. Navigate the results by page to see where the acronym is first used and ensure that the term it stands for is not repeated elsewhere in the document.

Capitalisation

When you're unsure whether to capitalise a word, ask yourself whether it's a common noun or proper noun. Common nouns don't need to be capitalised; proper nouns do. Proper nouns include the names of people, organisations, institutions and products. Sometimes it's difficult to know when a word is being used as a proper noun and when as a common noun. Here are some guidelines:

- When a title is attached to an individual, use upper case: President Cyril Ramaphosa. But when it stands alone, use lower case: the president.
- The names of official institutions and bodies are capitalised: Parliament, Morris Isaacson High School, the Department of Energy, the Finance and Audit Committee. But as common nouns, these terms take lower case. So, "state departments are being restructured", "I went to a high school in Port Elizabeth" and "The committee will consider the applications".
- "Constitution" is always upper case, but not "constitutional" (because it's an adjective). "Act" and "Bill" are capitalised when attached to specific legislation – for example, the Children's Act, the Bill of Rights. But "the act" or "the bill" is lower case when it's not part of a formal name.

Overcapitalisation confuses the reader and makes your writing hard to follow. The underlined words in the following example should all be in lower case:

> You can choose to have your Annual Service Charge, Financial Adviser Annual Service Charge and Portfolio Management Fee deducted from your Investment Portfolio, which you can change at any time.

Using capitalisation to emphasise a point comes across as aggressive or rude (the reader might think you're SHOUTING at them). Rather use bold, but don't overdo it.

Graphs, tables and figures

Some information is best presented visually. Graphics can often capture information more effectively than sentences, but, like writing, they require work to be clear and informative. When you're working with graphs, tables, figures and infographics it helps to consider these questions:

- What is the graphic's purpose?
- How does it add value?
- How does it relate to the text?
- Is the key message clear?

A rule of thumb: if the graphic needs a lot of explanation, it's not very useful. Avoid simply describing what the graphic shows, which defeats its purpose. It should be sufficient to introduce the graphic with an explanatory line or draw attention to a key feature of what is being portrayed.

When you're at the airport looking at the departures and arrivals board, you don't read everything displayed there. Instead, you search for the information that is most relevant to you. Apply the same principle when you're writing about graphics: direct the reader's attention to significant details. Also ensure you get the basics right, such as providing clear labels, units of measurement and the source of your data (if necessary). We give a few examples on the following pages.

Example 1

This table is taken from Australia's 2018/19 federal budget.[52] It's long and complicated, with a lot of information contained in the notes. In addition, the information is not shown consistently – for example, decimals are used in the second column, but fractions are used thereafter – making it even more difficult for the reader to understand the information quickly.

Table 1: Domestic economy forecasts(a)

	Outcomes(b)	Forecasts		
	2016-17	2017-18	2018-19	2019-20
Real gross domestic product	**2.1**	**2 3/4**	**3**	**3**
Household consumption	**2.6**	2 3/4	2 3/4	3
Dwelling investment	**2.8**	-3	1 1/2	0
Total business investment(c)	**-4.0**	4 1/2	3	4 1/2
By industry				
Mining investment	**-24.2**	-11	-7	3 1/2
Non-mining investment	**6.1**	10 1/2	5 1/2	5
Private final demand(c)	**1.4**	2 1/2	2 1/2	3
Public final demand(c)	**5.1**	4 3/4	3	2 3/4
Change in inventories(d)	**0.1**	- 1/4	0	0
Gross national expenditure	**2.4**	3	2 3/4	3
Exports of goods and services	**5.5**	2 1/2	4	2 1/2
Imports of goods and services	**4.9**	5	2	2 1/2
Net exports(d)	**0.0**	- 1/2	1/4	0
Nominal gross domestic product	**5.9**	4 1/4	3 3/4	4 3/4
Prices and wages				
Consumer price index(e)	**1.9**	2	2 1/4	2 1/2
Wage price index(f)	**1.9**	2 1/4	2 3/4	3 1/4
GDP deflator	**3.8**	1 3/4	3/4	1 1/2
Labour market				
Participation rate (per cent)(g)	**65.0**	65 1/2	65 1/2	65 1/2
Employment(f)	**1.9**	2 3/4	1 1/2	1 1/2
Unemployment rate (per cent)(g)	**5.6**	5 1/2	5 1/4	5 1/4
Balance of payments				
Terms of trade(h)	**14.4**	1 1/2	-5 1/4	-2 1/4
Current account balance (per cent of GDP)	**-2.1**	-2 1/4	-2 3/4	-3 1/4

(a) Percentage change on preceding year unless otherwise indicated.
(b) Calculated using original data unless otherwise indicated.
(c) Excluding second-hand asset sales from the public sector to the private sector.
(d) Percentage point contribution to growth in GDP.
(e) Through-the-year growth rate to the June quarter.
(f) Seasonally adjusted, through-the-year growth rate to the June quarter.
(g) Seasonally adjusted rate for the June quarter.
(h) The forecasts are underpinned by price assumptions for key commodities: Iron ore spot price remaining at US$55/tonne free-on-board (FOB); metallurgical coal spot price falling over the June and September quarters of 2018 to reach US$120/tonne FOB by the December 2018 quarter; and the thermal coal spot price remaining at US$93/tonne FOB.

Note: The forecasts for the domestic economy are based on several technical assumptions. The exchange rate is assumed to remain around its recent average level — a trade-weighted index of around 63 and a US$ exchange rate of around 77 US cents. Interest rates are assumed to move broadly in line with market expectations. World oil prices (Malaysian Tapis) are assumed to remain around US$71 per barrel.
Source: ABS cat. no. 5206.0, 5302.0, 6202.0, 6345.0, 6401.0, unpublished ABS data and Treasury.

52 Commonwealth of Australia, *Budget Strategy and Outlook*, Budget Paper No. 1, 2018–19, Statement 2, p. 6.

Example 2

For comparison, consider the table below, which is taken from South Africa's 2018 *Budget Review*.[53] It contains less information than the previous example and is far more readable. This is largely because space is used more effectively, the formatting is clean and consistent, and there is a good balance between analysis and data. The summary sentence to the left, in grey italics, usefully highlights a key point.

Domestic outlook

GDP growth is expected at 1.5 per cent in 2018 and at 1.8 per cent in 2019

The South African economy is forecast to grow by 1.5 per cent in 2018 and by 1.8 per cent in 2019. On average, the growth outlook is 0.4 percentage points higher than projected in October 2017, mainly due to an expected increase in private investment as a result of improved business and consumer confidence.

CHAPTER 2: ECONOMIC OVERVIEW

Table 2.2 Macroeconomic performance and projections

	2014	2015	2016	2017	2018	2019	2020
Percentage change		**Actual**		**Estimate**		**Forecast**	
Final household consumption	0.7	1.7	0.8	1.3	1.7	1.9	2.3
Final government consumption	1.1	0.5	2.0	0.0	-0.3	1.2	1.4
Gross fixed-capital formation	1.7	2.3	-3.9	0.3	1.9	3.3	3.7
Gross domestic expenditure	0.6	1.8	-0.8	1.3	1.7	2.2	2.4
Exports	3.2	3.9	-0.1	1.5	3.8	3.4	3.5
Imports	-0.5	5.4	-3.7	2.7	4.4	4.6	4.5
Real GDP growth	**1.7**	**1.3**	**0.3**	**1.0**	**1.5**	**1.8**	**2.1**
GDP inflation	5.8	5.0	7.0	4.9	5.7	5.3	5.5
GDP at current prices (R billion)	**3 807.7**	**4 049.8**	**4 345.8**	**4 604.4**	**4 940.8**	**5 298.3**	**5 704.6**
CPI inflation	6.1	4.6	6.3	5.3	5.3	5.4	5.5
Current account balance (% of GDP)	-5.3	-4.4	-3.3	-2.2	-2.3	-2.7	-3.2

Source: National Treasury and Reserve Bank

53 National Treasury, Republic of South Africa, 2018 *Budget Review*, pp. 16–17.

Example 3

The slide below is taken from the South African Reserve Bank's *Monetary Policy Review* presentation for April 2020.[54] It's a good example of how to tell a story through concise use of text and graphics. At the top, the slide's title summarises the general point. The slide is well balanced with two graphics that are aligned and formatted consistently. The information they contain is not too detailed and the key points are easily accessible, thanks to each graph's heading and red text highlighting the focal point.

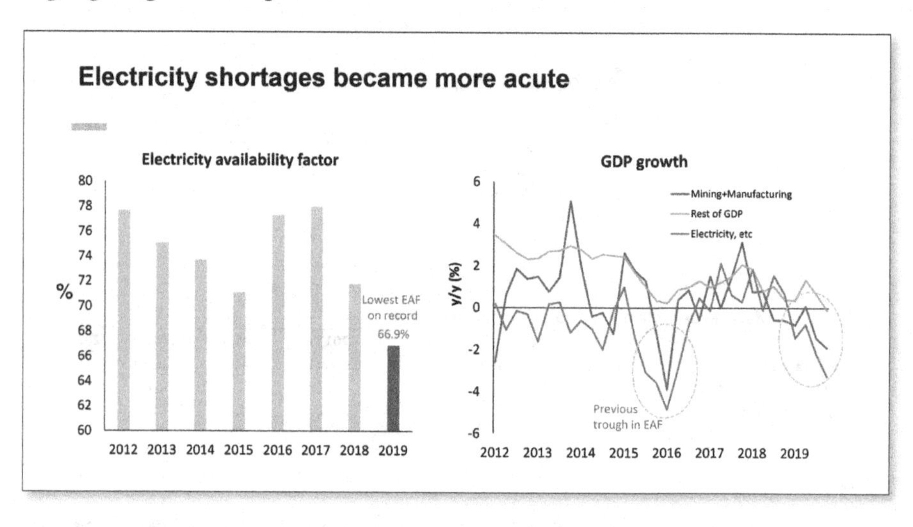

In the graph on the left, the value of greatest interest is for the current year, which is why the last bar is highlighted in red and accompanied by a caption explaining that this is the lowest value on record (red here signifies that this is cause for concern). The measures of electricity availability for the other years are omitted as they are not as important as the simple comparison of bar height for the period under review. The vertical bar graph is a good choice for the content as the reader will intuitively grasp that greater availability of electricity (higher bars) is better.

The graph on the right makes good use of bright, contrasting colours for the graph lines. The two yellow circles focus the reader's attention on the low points of GDP growth, with the caption in red text prompting the reader to compare the current situation with the last trough. It doesn't take much effort to absorb the main points of these two graphs before moving on.

54 South African Reserve Bank, Presentation of the *Monetary Policy Review*, April 2020, slide 22.

Example 4

When you have a set of data that you'd like to visualise, your guiding question should be: What key message do I want to communicate? The answer will inform the kind of graphic you choose to represent your data and how you put it together, including how you label it. If you don't ask yourself this question, you could end up with data packaged in an unsuitable format, where the reader is left wondering what message they're supposed to take away.

Consider the graphs below. They're drawn from a report on the perceived positive impact of increasing internet connectivity in Sub-Saharan Africa.[55]

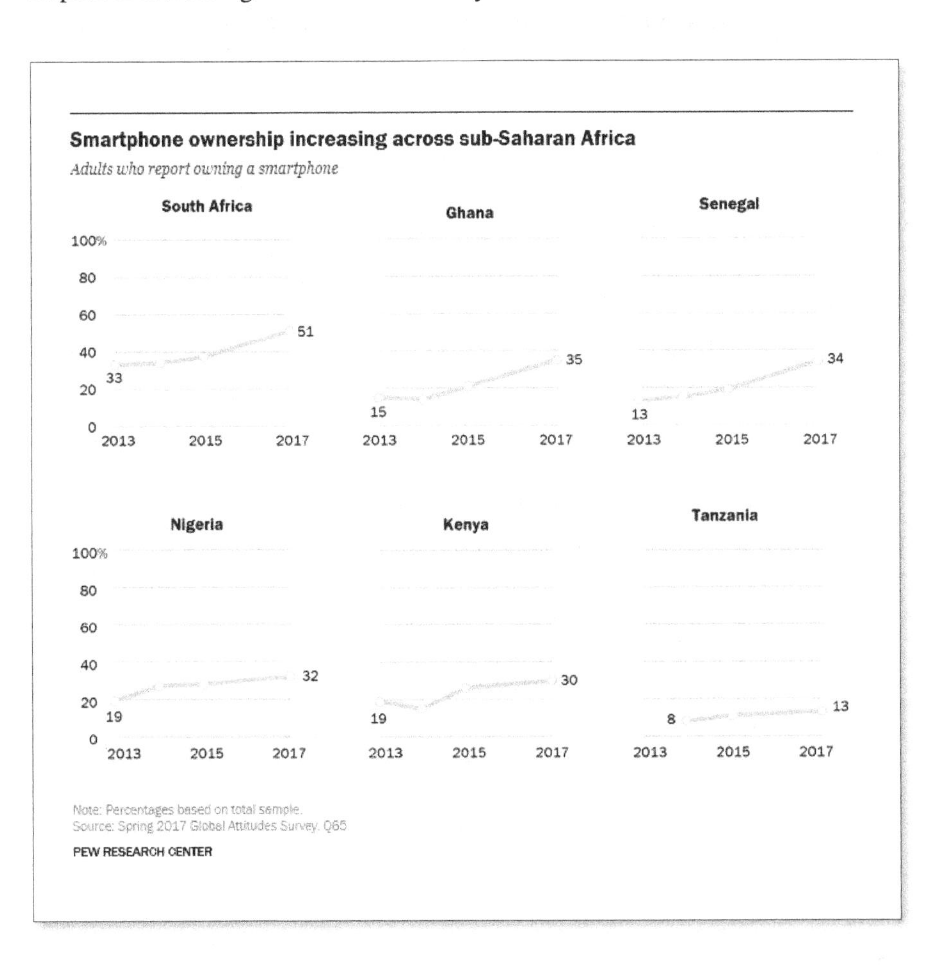

55 Laura Silver and Courtney Johnson, *Internet Connectivity Seen as Having Positive Impact on Life in Sub-Saharan Africa*, p. 13.

The purpose of this graphic seems to be twofold: one, to compare smartphone ownership in six African countries over a period of five years, and two, to isolate the figures per country. But if the period and unit of measurement (percentage of adults per country who report using a smartphone) are the same, why not consolidate the information into a single graph and clarify the focus? If you're primarily interested in comparing uptake of smartphones over the five-year period, then a graph like the one below would work better, allowing you to plot the trends and distinguish them with colours.

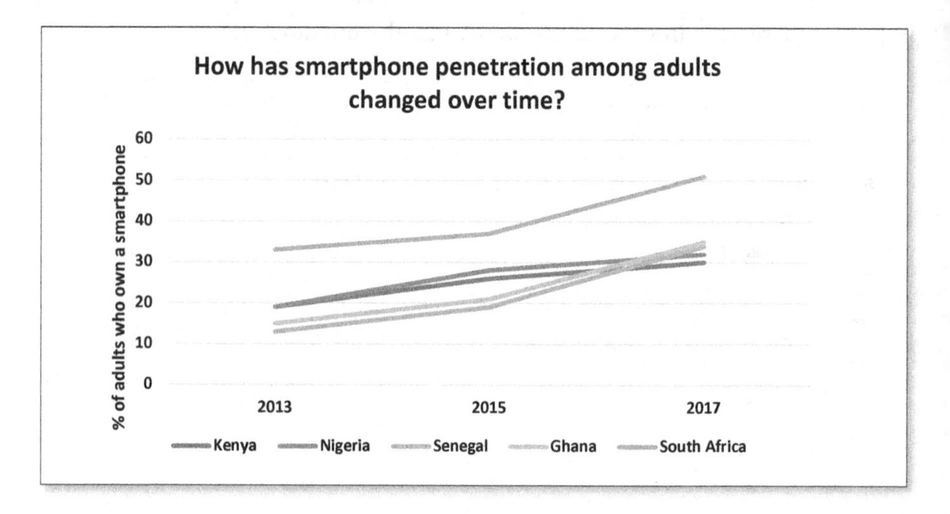

If you're more interested in isolating smartphone penetration in a single year, then the following graph would work well.

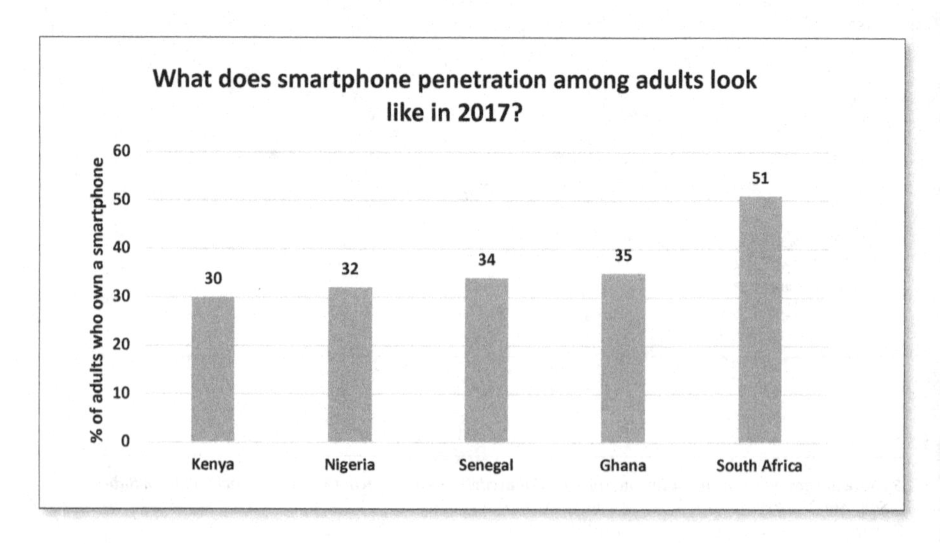

The two graphs are based on the same dataset but highlight different key messages. You could also rely on the first graph to understand smartphone penetration in 2017 – for instance, by inserting a value for 2017 at the tip of each graph line – but it's easier to understand through the second graph. Notice how each graphic answers the question posed in the heading.

In sum, for an effective graphic, you need to choose the correct kind of graphic, ensure accuracy and provide clean design and clear labelling – but the crucial first step is to figure out what message you want the graphic to communicate.

To wrap up

When you're listening to a persuasive person speak, you're not always conscious of what makes their words persuasive. While it may seem like a kind of magic trick, it's really a matter of getting the basics right.

As we've seen in this chapter, how you present your writing is not just a cosmetic consideration. Well-ordered presentation ensures the reader can focus on your content without distraction. Sensible paragraphing and good use of logical connectors support coherence and the flow of ideas. Emphasising key ideas with devices like bullets helps enhance the clarity of your writing. And, as we've just seen, similar considerations of clarity, concision and accessibility apply when you're working with graphics.

But an eye for correctness is not all: you need to organise your words and visualise your information in an engaging way. This requires keeping a close eye on details while not forgetting to step back to think about the text as a whole. The next chapter is devoted to this aspect of writing.

CHAPTER 4

Editing

A crucial part of becoming a better writer is looking at your work with a critical eye to correct errors and eliminate weaknesses. The novelist Zadie Smith advises writers to "read your own work as a stranger would read it, or even better, as an enemy would".[56] A stranger or an enemy would not be sympathetic to mistakes and clumsiness. You need to earn your reader's respect by ensuring your words are well chosen. Writing gets you halfway to where you want to be; editing completes the job.

What is editing and why do it?

Editing is many things. It's reshuffling, rethinking, reformulating, restructuring, rewriting. It's scanning a sentence for weaknesses of various kinds: words that are not quite right, gaps in logic, too much or too little detail, poor flow, a jarring tone, faulty grammar, missing punctuation. It's "listening" for the sound and sense of a sentence, and fine-tuning it. It's tidying up loose threads so that your text is consistently presented. It's deciding whether it's more appropriate to write "it is" or "it's" – for reasons of tone, space or flow.

At the most basic level, editing is about good housekeeping, keeping your sentences clean and shipshape. Random House copy chief Benjamin Dreyer points out that this involves "shaking loose and rearranging punctuation ... and keeping an eye open for dropped words ('He went to store') and repeated words ('He went to the the store') and other glitches that take root during writing and revision". But it's also about *craft*: finding a way of making the key message in a piece ring clear. "On a good day," Dreyer writes, editing "achieves something between a really thorough teeth cleaning ... and a whiz-bang magic act".[57]

---

56 Zadie Smith, "Zadie Smith's rules for writers", *The Guardian*, 22 February 2010.

57 Benjamin Dreyer, *Dreyer's English*, p. xii.

Editing is not just about ensuring that your writing complies with all the rules of grammar and punctuation. It's also about taking a bird's-eye view and looking for ways to make your work clearer, and more coherent and fluent. It involves weeding out unnecessary words and cutting to the heart of the matter, so that your main points stand clear.

"Whenever you feel an impulse to perpetrate a piece of exceptionally fine writing, obey it – wholeheartedly – and delete it before sending your manuscript to press. Murder your darlings." This quote is often misattributed to William Faulkner, the American novelist. In fact, it comes from a lecture on writing delivered at Cambridge University in 1914 by Arthur Quiller-Couch, an English literary critic.

Both the quote's misattribution and its content are the point: when you're editing, it's as important to get your facts right as it is to get rid of waffle. You may be reluctant to cut away words that you've laboured to find or get just right. Or you hesitate to remove some not-entirely-relevant sentences because they sound melodious or show how widely you've read around your topic. It can be hard to give your own words the chop, which is why Stephen King is only slightly exaggerating when he says that "to write is human, to edit is divine".[58]

So, why should we edit? Because good writing depends on it.

The bird's-eye view

Details matter – but so does the bigger picture. Ensuring that the nuts and bolts of your sentences are in place is important, but it's just as important to take a broader view of your piece of writing: how it opens, how it flows, how it ends.

When you've got your first draft, before you fixate on the finer details like where to place a comma or whether to use brackets or a dash, step back. If you were working on a painting, at this point you'd stand back from the canvas and regard the overall composition. This is how you begin a structural, or substantive, edit.

Start at the top with your title. The title is the hook that catches your reader's attention. Consider it provisional until you've finished writing the body of your piece, as your focus may shift along the way.

58 Stephen King, third Foreword to *On Writing*, p. 20.

After the title, edit the opening section. These precious lines should introduce the topic and highlight key issues. Your ability to draw the reader in is likely to rest on a solid opening paragraph.

Imagine you're employed by an engineering firm. You've been asked to write a column for a national business newspaper in which you make the case for further investment in water storage and distribution systems across southern Africa. To underline the urgency of such projects, you know you'll need to present some striking facts. But facts alone won't hook your reader's attention. You need something more.

Consider the two approaches below.

Example 1

> Water can catalyse wealth creation but also drive conflict. Over 95 million people share water from 15 river basins in southern Africa. Twenty-eight million of these people lack reliable access to water – a major driver of extreme poverty.

Example 2

> Water is life. Its presence helps people improve their lives; its absence means poverty. Over 95 million people share water from 15 river basins in southern Africa and 28 million of them lack reliable access to water.

In example 1, the first sentence lacks urgency. The verbs "catalyse" and "drive" are abstract and "can" is a word that frames possibilities rather than a current reality. Example 2, in contrast, starts with a simple declarative sentence. It is stronger than "Water is essential for life". The second sentence uses juxtaposition (enabled by a semicolon) to illustrate the importance of water. We then proceed into the narrower focus of statistics relating to southern Africa.

There's little difference between the factual content of the two examples, but a significant difference in emotional pitch. And if all that seems too complicated, read the first sentence of each out loud. That should settle the matter. A strong opening is how you grab your reader's attention.

Here's another example, on the importance of developing enhanced rainfed agriculture in Africa:

> Africa is facing a crisis. One-third of people across the continent are food insecure. Two-thirds of the population are trapped in a cycle of poverty, exacerbated by climate change and rapidly rising population growth. Water is an increasingly scarce resource. At the centre of this crisis is the African farmer, typically engaged in rainfed subsistence farming.

What makes this opening effective is the short, focused sentences. They sketch the nature of the problem and then zoom in on the focus of the study: the African farmer. Having provided the context, the writer can go on to expand on these elements in separate paragraphs – defining rainfed agriculture, giving an overview of food production in Africa, discussing relevant initiatives and outlining the structure of the fuller discussion.

Once you have a strong opening, focus your attention on how the parts of your piece fit together. If your sections have headings, check that they are concise and arranged logically. Ideally, your headings should map the key components of your message or stages of your argument. In a longer document, the table of contents should provide an accurate snapshot of your content. Check your paragraphs for length and coherence. Look out for patches of discussion that digress from the topic or are unnecessarily dense. Scan your work for unexplained assumptions, undefined terms and gaps in logic.

Look carefully at how your piece ends. Is your discussion complete? Have you provided the reader with all the relevant information? Most importantly, are the key messages clear? If so, you can then proceed to copy edit your sentences, checking for grammatical correctness and clarity.

WHAT'S THE DIFFERENCE BETWEEN PROOFREADING, COPY EDITING AND SUBSTANTIVE EDITING?

There are different grades of editing, ranging from a light edit or proofread, through a standard copy edit, to the more rigorous substantive or structural edit.

Proofreading involves reviewing a document for errors and inconsistencies. It includes checking spelling, grammar and aspects of formatting (such as line spacing and numerical order), correcting typographical errors ("typos") and ensuring stylistic consistency. Proofreading is often best done after a copy edit to ensure an error-free text. Unlike copy editing and substantive editing, final proofreading should be done on paper.

Copy editing is a standard check of an entire document to ensure it's clear, free of errors and makes sense. Language is tightened, sentences are shortened and grammatical, syntactical and punctuation errors are fixed. The editor looks for ways to improve how ideas are presented, for example by querying statements that are confusing or contradictory, calling out or removing repetition, and revising passive voice formulations to the active voice. The document's style is also checked to ensure that there's consistency in capitalisation, font usage and size, presentation of numbers and so on. In North America and Europe, many publishing houses, media outlets and large organisations employ fact-checkers. Few organisations in southern Africa do so. Nevertheless, a good copy editor will keep an eye out for factual errors or inconsistencies, and check the veracity of statements where feasible.

Substantive (or structural) editing is more thorough than a standard copy edit and involves bringing a strategic eye to the text. The editor conducts a high-level review of the whole document to ensure its structure makes sense – from chapters, sections and paragraphs to key messages within paragraphs. Messages are interrogated and sentences are often rewritten entirely to ensure the main idea is presented as clearly and accessibly as possible. Suggestions may be made to the author to remove entire sections or add content where there are gaps. Questions of tone, relevance and the audience are front of mind throughout the edit.

Punctuation and grammar essentials

Punctuation can mean the difference between life and death, as we can see from this commonly used example:

> Let's eat, Grandma.
>
> Let's eat Grandma.

While in this one we have two very different resolutions:

> I'm giving up drinking for a month.
>
> I'm giving up. Drinking for a month.

Punctuation is not optional – it's essential for giving your sentences the intended meaning and ensuring they fit together well.

In her book *Eats, Shoots & Leaves: The Zero Tolerance Approach to Punctuation* (2003), Lynne Truss compares punctuation to politeness: "Truly good manners are invisible: they ease the way for others, without drawing attention to themselves."[59] Similarly, punctuation should help the reader understand a piece of writing while going unnoticed.

Although social media encourages us to sacrifice it for the sake of speed, punctuation is not a kind of spice that you can choose to sprinkle over your sentences to give them more flavour. Used carefully, it can enhance the clarity of your writing, making it punchier – as in the following example.

> The opinion **of the** manager **of the** content **of the** report was clear.
>
> The <u>manager's</u> opinion of the <u>report's</u> content was clear.

The deft use of apostrophes in this example allows us to remove the clunky repetition of "of the" and set up a clear relationship between the subject of the sentence ("the manager") and the object ("the report's content").

Punctuation errors can have costly consequences. Sometimes the cost is financial. One case involving delivery truck drivers and an ambiguously placed comma cost a dairy company in the US state of Maine some $5 million. The

59 Lynne Truss, *Eats, Shoots & Leaves*, pp. 7–8.

drivers' argument that they qualified for overtime pay hinged on a comma – or rather the lack of one. The state's law stipulates that the following activities do **not** qualify for overtime pay:

> The canning, processing, preserving, freezing, drying, marketing, storing, packing for shipment or distribution of:
>
> (1) Agricultural produce;
>
> (2) Meat and fish products; and
>
> (3) Perishable foods.

The drivers argued that the lack of a comma after "shipment" means that the law applies to the activity of *packing* (for shipment or distribution) rather than *distribution* as a distinct activity. Because the drivers' work did not involve packing at all, they would qualify for overtime pay. And so we have the case of the $5 million comma.[60]

Your reputation can also take a hit when you misuse punctuation. Don't be like Donald Trump Junior and misplace the apostrophe in the subtitle of your book: it doesn't look good. *Liberal Privilege: Joe Biden and the Democrat's Defense of the Indefensible* is the title Trump's book was initially given. But shortly before its publication in August 2020, the apostrophe in the subtitle was moved to after the "s".[61] After all, the president's son, who is not known for his tact or concern for accuracy, did not mean to target just one Democrat but all Democrats. If you plan to attack a target, at least be sure to get your target right.

Using punctuation correctly is a sign that you respect your reader. It also shows that you understand that a clear message depends not just on your choice and arrangement of words, but on attention to the detail of how those words appear on the page. In this section, we'll refresh your knowledge of a few punctuation essentials. We'll also touch on errors of concord.

---

60 Daniel Victor, "Oxford comma dispute is settled as Maine drivers get $5 million", *New York Times*, 9 February 2018.

61 Alison Flood, "Donald Trump Jr tries to tidy up his book Liberal Privilege's grammar", *The Guardian*, 29 July 2020.

Apostrophes

Some writers, unsure how to correctly use apostrophes, apply them randomly and hope for the best. Mastering the use of the apostrophe is a small but crucial step towards making the relationships between words in your sentence clear and logical.

It's a small punctuation mark that makes a big difference. Consider the fundamental difference in the oft-cited example of a business that knows its shit, versus a business that knows it's shit.

So, know your apostrophes!

The apostrophe shows either possession or contraction.

To show possession

Form the possessive singular of nouns and proper nouns by adding an **'s**. For example, Dumisa's phone, Gabriel's bike, Dr Erasmus's assistant. When a name ends in an **s**, some people just use the apostrophe rather than the apostrophe plus the **s** (so, Dr Erasmus' assistant). This holds for ancient proper names that end in **-us**, **-es** or **-is**: Jesus' disciples, Moses' followers, Artemis' temple. But if you want to be safe, make a habit of including both the apostrope and the **s**, regardless of whether the name ends in **s** or not.

For nouns that are already in the plural and end with **s**, only an apostrophe is required. For example, the ladies' hats, the ministers' policies, the companies' representatives. For plural nouns that don't end in **s**, you apply the same rule as that for singular nouns. For example, the crowd's cheers, the children's laughter, the people's objections.

Note that possessive pronouns like *hers, his, its, theirs, yours* and *ours* take no apostrophe. So, we write "The table top has lost **its** shine" and "That book is not mine, it's **hers**". In these two examples, notice the difference between "its" and "it's". The apostrophe in "it's" always indicates a contraction of "it is".

To show contraction

The other purpose of the apostrophe is to mark where a word has been contracted and a letter left out. Examples include "isn't", "doesn't", "wasn't", "hasn't", "didn't" and "wouldn't".

WRONG	WHY?	RIGHT
The dog wagged it's tail.	***An English oddity (one of many) is that "it's" is a contraction of "it is", but "its" means of or relating to it or itself***	The dog wagged its tail.
The travel package includes optional extra's.	***Apostrophes don't mark plurals***	The travel package includes optional extras.

Commas

The comma is one of the most misused punctuation marks, which is unsurprising given that it's also the most commonly used. The title of the book *Eats, Shoots & Leaves* is taken from a joke that illustrates the confusion that can arise from a misplaced comma:

> A panda walks into a café, orders a sandwich, eats it, then pulls out a gun and fires two shots in the air. He then begins to leave. A perplexed waiter asks "Why?" The panda thrusts a wildlife book at the waiter, saying, "I'm a panda. Look it up." Under the entry, the waiter finds: "Panda. Large black-and-white bear-like mammal, native to China. Eats, shoots and leaves."[62]

Tightening up your sentences starts with understanding where to place your commas. The purpose of a comma is to help a reader understand how the parts of a sentence fit together to create a particular meaning. Too many commas can clutter a sentence and cause confusion.

Here are a few useful guidelines.

Lists

Use a comma to separate a series of items. For example: "I bought apples, oranges and pears." A comma is unnecessary after "oranges" unless you're using the serial (or Oxford) comma, which separates the last two items in a list ("I bought apples, oranges, and pears"). The serial comma is helpful when there are more than three items in the list and a number of "ands". For example, "I went to the shop and bought apples and oranges, milk and yoghurt, and bread and biscuits." Here, the items have been grouped by category (fruit, dairy

62 Lynne Truss, *Eats, Shoots & Leaves*, rear dustcover.

products and baked goods). Similarly, in the following example, commas help to separate different categories:

> Since 2008, large drops in productivity have been recorded in mining, footwear and textiles, fibre and rubber products, electricity and water supply, construction, transport, and non-financial private services.

A semicolon (which we'll shortly discuss in more detail) makes the list even clearer:

> Since 2008, large drops in productivity have been recorded in mining; footwear and textiles; fibre and rubber products; electricity and water supply; construction; transport; and non-financial private services.

Parenthesis

Commas are useful for including extra information about a subject in a sentence. If this information is presented as an aside, then we refer to it as being "in parenthesis" ("parentheses" is another name for round brackets, but parenthetical clauses can be set off by commas, brackets or dashes). When deciding whether extra information in a sentence requires commas on either side of it, ask yourself two questions:

1. Does the information define the subject (is it essential)? If it is essential – i.e. defining – then no commas are needed. That is why only the third sentence below is correct:

- Men like Mandela, are icons
- Men, like Mandela, are icons.
- Men like Mandela are icons.

You don't need commas in this sentence because "like Mandela" is defining what kind of man is an icon (it is an essential detail).

2. Does the sentence make sense if you ignore the clause between commas? In the following two examples, the answer is yes:

- The audience, which at first had been noisy, became quieter as the show went on.
- Durban, which had heavy rains recently, is a humid port city.

There's no hard rule for when to use a comma before an independent clause (a phrase that is grammatically complete). You need to use your judgement, paying attention to logic and flow. For example, both of the following sentences would make sense without commas, but it doesn't hurt to include them:

- My grandfather is old, but he still enjoys jogging.
- I know who you're talking about, although I haven't met her.

Here, the commas help to show where the opening statement is qualified. In a similar kind of sentence that is longer, the comma provides a pause as well as marking a step in logic. For example:

> Not only do the Sustainable Development Goals set targets for universal access to water and the elimination of open defecation, but they move beyond simple definitions of access to consider service quality.

Other common errors, and their solutions, appear in the examples below.

WRONG	WHY?	RIGHT
A key element of a good business strategy is, clear communication with customers.	***This sentence is a single statement and so should not be interrupted with a comma***	A key element of a good business strategy is clear communication with customers.
Digital shopping which is fast and convenient is becoming the norm.	***The phrase introduced by "which" provides extra information about the subject, so it needs to be enclosed between commas***	Digital shopping, which is fast and convenient, is becoming the norm.
Anyone, who wants to advance their career, should take advantage of on-the-job training.	***The phrase introduced by "who" is defining "anyone" and therefore should not be bracketed with commas***	Anyone who wants to advance their career should take advantage of on-the-job training.

Exceptions

You don't need to use a comma if two parts of a sentence are closely related. For example, no comma is needed before "and" in this example:

> She has many friends and is always happy to meet new people.

Similarly, don't join independent clauses with a comma. Doing so results in a run-on sentence like:

> It's nearly five o'clock, we will have to finish this work tomorrow.

In this case, it's better to use a full stop to form two sentences or to join the clauses with a coordinator like "as", "so" or "therefore". Rephrased, that example will read:

> It's nearly five o'clock, so we will have to finish this work tomorrow.

Hyphens and dashes

The hyphen and the dash are easily confused. But there is a simple difference in their function: **the hyphen joins multiple words to form a single word, whereas the dash separates parts of a sentence, much like a comma does.** The dash is longer than the hyphen. Before we get into a bit more detail on both, here's an illustration of the difference between them – a quote from Zakes Mda's novel *The Zulus of New York* (1999):

> His Zulu colleagues called him Mpi, which has become Em-Pee to the English-speakers. It is less punishing to the inexperienced tongue than Mpiyezintombi – Battle of the Maidens – so named because his father thought he was so handsome that women were going to fight over him.[63]

In the name "Em-Pee", the hyphen shows how the two syllables of the name are pronounced separately, while "English-speakers" is a noun formed from the longer phrase "speakers of English". The dash, meanwhile, provides an interruption for extra detail about the character's name.

Let's take a closer look.

63 Zakes Mda, *The Zulus of New York*, p. 18.

The hyphen for compound adjectives

A compound adjective consists of two words joined with a **hyphen**. The hyphen helps to distinguish the adjective from the noun it describes. Some examples:

- The **two-day** workshop will include four **panel-based** sessions.
- We'll have a **follow-up** session in two weeks.
- The **25-year-old** woman bought a **top-of-the-range** car.

In the first example, removing the hyphen opens the door to ambiguity because it's unclear if the workshop runs over two days ("a two-day workshop") or if there are two workshops, each lasting a day ("two day-workshops").

In some sentences with multiple words before the noun, it's difficult to know where to place the hyphen. Consider this sentence: "Lower middle income countries are facing economic difficulty." If you want to be clear that "lower-middle-income" is the adjective, you would hyphenate those three words. But it's also important to be aware of general usage. For example, it's not common practice to hyphenate "climate change" when it's used in a phrase like "climate change initiatives" because climate change is a common enough term that "climate change-initiatives" is an unlikely interpretation.

You don't need to hyphenate an adverb (which generally ends in -ly) when it occurs alongside a verb before a noun. The "-ly" does the job of a hyphen, indicating that it's modifying the word that follows. For example:

- The **rapidly** approaching train blew its whistle.
- Economists are making **increasingly** optimistic forecasts.

The dash for including extra detail or giving emphasis

The **dash** can be used to enclose extra information about the subject of the sentence or to emphasise a point. The dash marks out extra information in a slightly more definitive manner than commas. A few examples:

- Three of South Africa's universities – UCT, Wits and Stellenbosch – are ranked among the world's top 500 universities.
- I want to thank you for committing to this programme and I hope you see areas of your work – and your personal lives – where it will be useful.

You can also use a dash to introduce an illustration or claim. In the following examples, a comma could also be used but a dash gives more emphasis:

- Regular consumption of coffee was found to contribute to depression in adults – an unexpected result.
- The biology department will struggle to function efficiently and meet its targets – particularly if its budget is cut.

Colons and semicolons

Colons and semicolons are often confused. **Colons are generally used to introduce a list, explanation or example**:

> Ubuntu, Thawte and PayPal have more in common than meets the eye: not only are they pioneering software in the modern age of computing, but they were all created by South Africans.

Semicolons have two functions. The first is to **separate items in a list where each item consists of a long phrase.** In the following example, the semicolons demarcate the categories of item (IT equipment, linen and gardening materials); they are like major commas:

> I went shopping on Takealot and bought a flat-screen TV, speakers and a laptop; pillows, a duvet and sheets; and a lawnmower and gardening tools.

The second function of semicolons is to **separate two independent clauses that have an implied connection.** For example:

- The election results have not been finalised; votes are still being counted at polling stations across the country.
- Most South African startups operate at a small scale; few have international customers or ambitions to enter global markets.

Since semicolons are often misused for this purpose, we suggest you avoid using them until you're entirely confident you're using them correctly. Instead, play it safe: use a full stop and create two sentences.

Errors of concord

By "concord" we mean agreement. Errors of concord occur when two words in a sentence that should agree, don't. This kind of error is common, particularly between subject and verb, and usually involves the number of a word (i.e. whether it's singular or plural). Sometimes the error is clear, as in this sentence: "The **cost** of maintaining these properties **are** many times higher than the costs charged by private-sector firms." The word "cost" is singular so it should be used with the singular verb "is". Here, the writer has been misled into using "are" by the plural "properties".

Collective nouns should generally be treated as singular, as in these examples:

- The government has launched a number of projects to create jobs.
- A flock of geese is flying overhead.
- A crowd of people has gathered in the street.

In longer sentences where a parenthetical clause is involved, check that the subject and verb agree. Matching the number of the verb to the number of the subject is not always straightforward, particularly when there are other nouns of different number in the same sentence. For example:

- The CEO, as well as many other top managers, is on vacation.
- The new policies, unlike the one introduced last year, have proved effective.

With these sentences, the trick is to ensure that the phrase or clause adding a subject of a different number is fully enclosed between commas. This separates it from the outer clause and allows you to match the subject of the clause at the head of the sentence with the verb that completes it ("CEO ... is", "policies ... have"). Look out for nouns that seem to be plural but are treated as singular. For example, "Politics ~~are~~ is an art, not a science."

Use a singular verb with words like *each*, *either*, *neither*, *everyone*, *everybody*, *no one*, *nobody*, *someone* and *somebody*. Be careful with a word like *everyone*: many people are being referred to – but as individuals, not as a group. Some examples:

- Everyone is expected to arrive on time.
- No one likes to receive a poor performance review.
- Neither the municipality nor the province has formulated a drought disaster plan.

WRONG	RIGHT
The **projects focuses** on creating jobs and reducing poverty.	The projects focus on creating jobs and reducing poverty.
Neither **my brother** nor **my sister** are on holiday yet.	Neither my brother nor my sister is on holiday yet.
The **organisation have** made reducing its operating costs a priority.	The organisation has made reducing its operating costs a priority.

BE YOUR OWN EDITOR: THE BASICS

1. **REVIEW STRUCTURE, FLOW AND CLARITY**
   - Ensure the key messages are clear.
   - Shorten paragraphs and subheadings that are too long.
   - Check that all acronyms are defined and technical terms explained (where necessary).
   - Update the table of contents so that chapter titles, section headings and page numbers are accurate.
2. **RUN A SPELLING AND GRAMMAR CHECK**

   The automated spelling and grammar check in Microsoft Word highlights errors in your text and suggests corrections. Some of these "errors" are not in fact errors – you need to decide whether a change is warranted.
3. **CHECK THAT YOUR FONT AND LAYOUT ARE CONSISTENT**
   - Make sure you've used the same font style and size throughout.
   - Ensure consistent spacing between lines, headings and paragraphs.
   - Use the find/replace function to check for double spaces between words and replace them with single spaces.
   - Check that figures and tables have headings and are numbered, and that the axes of graphs are correctly labelled.
4. **PROOFREAD IN HARD COPY**

   Often, errors only come to light when you read your work in hard copy. Even if you've done what you think is a thorough on-screen edit, print out your document and check it for errors and oversights.

To wrap up

This chapter has focused on ensuring your content hangs together well and getting the mechanics of your sentences right. It can be difficult to do this when you're putting your thoughts into words for the first time. That's why, in the interest of getting a first draft done, it's best just to write without censoring yourself. Then you can rework and improve through editing.

Being your own editor first involves taking a wide-angle view so you can get an impression of your document's overall structure by reviewing aspects like paragraph and section length and subheadings. You should also pay attention to logical flow: how the storyline or argument is developed (more on this in the next chapter). When you're comfortable with the overall structure, focus on the nuts and bolts of your sentences – the punctuation and grammar – as well as how they hinge together to form paragraphs.

Writing to the point cuts across all these levels: word choice, sentence structure, paragraphing, document design. It's about weighing your words against your main ideas and finding a way of getting those ideas across most effectively. Doing so will ensure that the reader doesn't lose interest, which in today's attention economy is a crucial consideration.

CHAPTER 5

The advanced toolkit

The nuts and bolts of writing matter a great deal. Without vigorous verbs, notable nouns, alluring adjectives, artful adverbs and capable connectors, your elevated writing expectations are likely to be brought low. But mastery of the basics is just the first step: you need to put it all together. This chapter covers more advanced approaches to develop the art and craft of writing: the strategic benefits of narrative, how to vary your style to maintain the reader's interest and ways of dealing with difficult topics.

Narrative and analogy

Narrative is how you bring your ideas together. It's especially useful if your subject matter is dense or technical. Stories make it easier for people to understand the interplay of complex factors and how these relate to their lives. The stories that leading political figures tell about their vision of how things should be can change the way people see themselves and behave. Think of Thabo Mbeki's "I am an African" speech or Martin Luther King's "I have a dream" speech.[64]

A story is more likely to engage and motivate an audience than a set of facts, statistics and quotations. Facts are abstract, whereas a story involves co-creation: I tell you a story about something and you form images and associations of your own. It's also easier to remember a story than a list of bullet points. A story is more likely to arouse emotions and have a personal resonance.

Here's an example. We all felt the effects of the 2008 global financial crisis, but how well do we grasp what happened? In a column published in the *Financial Times* in 2010, Martin Wolf did a good job of using a simple story about grasshoppers and ants to explain this complex event. These are the first three paragraphs:

---

64 Mbeki, at the time deputy president to Nelson Mandela, delivered this speech in Parliament in Cape Town on 8 May 1996 to mark the adoption of South Africa's new Constitution. King delivered his famous speech on the steps of the Lincoln Memorial in Washington, DC, on 28 August 1963 in front of some 250 000 supporters of the civil rights movement.

> Everybody in the west knows the fable of the grasshopper and the ant. The grasshopper is lazy and sings away the summer, while the ant piles up stores for the winter. When the cold weather comes, the grasshopper begs the ant for food. The ant refuses and the grasshopper starves. The moral of this story? Idleness brings want.
>
> Yet life is more complex than in Aesop's fable. Today, the ants are Germans, Chinese and Japanese, while the grasshoppers are American, British, Greek, Irish and Spanish. Ants produce enticing goods grasshoppers want to buy. The latter ask whether the former want something in return. "No," reply the ants. "You do not have anything we want, except, maybe, a spot by the sea. We will lend you the money. That way, you enjoy our goods and we accumulate stores."
>
> Ants and grasshoppers are happy. Being frugal and cautious, the ants deposit their surplus earnings in supposedly safe banks, which relend to grasshoppers. The latter, in turn, no longer need to make goods, since ants supply them so cheaply. But ants do not sell them houses, shopping malls or offices. So grasshoppers make these, instead. They even ask ants to come and do the work. Grasshoppers find that with all the money flowing in, the price of land rises. So they borrow more, build more and spend more.[65]

You may not want to use narrative in such an obvious way. Moreover, your material might be too technical or contain too many moving parts to render as a simple story. Nonetheless, a well-placed image or analogy can play an important role in clarifying your ideas and making them more accessible.

On matters of social urgency like climate change, a simple image is a good way of calling for a change in behaviour. An example is the story of the "hole in the ozone layer", a phenomenon that scientists targeted for action in the 1980s and 1990s. The ozone "hole" is not actually a hole but an area with an extreme depletion of ozone in the stratosphere over the Antarctic that becomes most evident around August each year.[66]

---

65 Martin Wolf, "The grasshoppers and the ants", *Financial Times*, 25 May 2010.

66 National Aeronautics Space Administration, "What is the Ozone Hole?".

In the story of the ozone layer, the main character is the earth being harmed by ultraviolet light that penetrates the atmosphere. Normally, the ozone layer would protect the earth's inhabitants from this dangerous radiation, but this protective layer has been depleted by chemicals called chlorofluorocarbons (CFCs), which are used in aerosol sprays and refrigerators. Reducing our use of CFCs allows the protective barrier of ozone to rebuild itself. The science about the ozone layer may be complex but the message about what we can do to combat the problem – don't use CFCs – is simple enough for people to understand and act on.

Another good, local example is Day Zero – the day when most of Cape Town's water taps would be switched off. In early 2018, the city introduced the idea of this terminal date to motivate its residents to limit their consumption of water to 50 litres per person per day. The date was not fixed but moved as the city monitored the effect of water rationing. The prospect of having to queue at public collection points for a daily allowance of 25 litres of water was a powerful motivator for people to change their water-consumption habits.

Your material may lack any obvious dramatic potential, but a carefully chosen image, metaphor or analogy can go a long way to making your points accessible to a wider audience. Here's an extract from a speech delivered by the governor of the South African Reserve Bank, Lesetja Kganyago, in January 2019:

> The financial sector plays an important intermediation role in the economy. ... Financial intermediaries and financial markets play this role by moving funds throughout the economy that in turn affect businesses and the production of goods and services. A financial system is therefore the lifeblood of a modern economy.[67]

We all know how blood works in the body, and so Kganyago uses this image to illustrate the vital mediating role that organisations like banks play in the economy. Note that he doesn't just refer to "blood" but "lifeblood", a slight but significant difference in emphasis. There's a lot more he could say about "financial intermediaries", but this is a good starting point for a speech to an audience that may include interested listeners who are not experts in finance and economics.

67 Delivered at the meeting of the Basel Committee on Banking Supervision and the Financial Stability Institute.

Prefer the concrete to the abstract

It's useful to think of narrative more broadly as describing events involving someone or something acting on something else with some result. As noted in Chapter 2 under principle 7 (Be specific), the way to make abstract subject matter engaging is to avoid abstract words and instead describe actors, actions and objects. The agent may not be human – for example, an enzyme, an insect or an interest rate. In the examples below, the passages on the left are difficult to understand because of the abstract nouns (underlined) they contain. The versions on the right are free of abstract padding and clearly identify actors and actions.

ABSTRACT	MORE CONCRETE AND DIRECT
I doubt that criminalising the sale of cigarettes would succeed **on an actual level**, although it is admirable from an **aspirational perspective**.	I doubt that criminalising the sale of cigarettes would succeed, although it is an admirable aspiration.
The issue of theft of copper cables **is a factor adding to the difficult conditions facing** our public rail system. We need partnership **strategies** involving rail company **interventions** as well as **initiatives** from a community involvement **perspective.**	Theft of copper cables is crippling our public rail system. We need to address the problem through partnerships between the rail company and community groups.

Beware of padding a passage with words like "level", "perspective", "issue", "condition" and "intervention". They take up space without providing useful conceptual grip, which makes them difficult to engage with when used in this way.

The direct or indirect approach?

Earlier we spoke about the importance of placing the main idea up front, not just in a sentence but in a paragraph. This is a good general rule to follow, but sometimes it can be more effective to hook the reader's interest indirectly.

In journalism, an introduction or "lead" to a story can be direct or indirect.[68] A **direct** lead tells the reader the most important aspect of the story at once. Here's an example:

> A weight-loss pill has been hailed as a potential "holy grail" in the fight against obesity after a major study showed it did not increase the risk of serious heart problems. Researchers say lorcaserin is the first weight-loss drug to be deemed safe for heart health with long-term use. Taken twice a day, the drug is an appetite suppressant which works by stimulating brain chemicals to induce a feeling of fullness. A US study saw 12,000 people who were either obese or overweight given the pills or a placebo – with those who took the drug shedding an average of 4 kg in 40 months. Further analysis showed no big differences in tests for heart valve damage.[69]

Most breaking news stories begin in this way. In longer news stories and feature articles, the topic is introduced more slowly with what is known as an **indirect** (or **delayed** or **anecdotal**) lead. The aim is to entice the reader into the story by hinting at its contents. Often, this involves focusing on dialogue, people or events that imply a larger narrative. In the following example, the topic of the piece is only revealed at the end of the paragraph:

> When a Chinese clothing company swooped in and offered to sponsor Kenya's famed runners, Nike panicked, Kenyan officials say. "Can we talk about the situation?" a Nike executive wrote to a Kenyan official after hearing the news that the Kenyans wanted to end their deal with Nike. "You and I go back a long way." What followed – according to email exchanges, letters, bank records and invoices, provided by a former employee of Kenya's athletics federation – has led to a major scandal in Kenya, a country in the midst of its biggest war against corruption in years.[70]

In this extract, the final sentence situates this story against the backdrop of corruption in Kenya while indicating the extensive body of evidence on which the story is based. The Chinese clothing company is not named, nor are the individuals, yet we are given a taste of the intrigue and conflict involved

---

68 The technical term is actually "lede", to distinguish it from the metal lead.

69 Press Association, "Weight-loss pill hailed as 'holy grail' in fight against obesity", *The Guardian*, 27 August 2018.

70 Jeffrey Gettleman, "Money given to Kenya, since stolen, puts Nike in spotlight", *New York Times*, 5 March 2016.

(key ingredients of a good story) – and the main topic is still introduced in the first paragraph.

Varying your style

Once you've mastered the principles of clear writing, you can start thinking about ways to liven up your prose.

Sentence length

To keep the reader interested, vary how you construct your sentences. If every sentence is short, declarative and in the active voice, your writing will become repetitive and boring. The writer Gary Provost demonstrates this point effectively:

> This sentence has five words. Here are five more words. Five-word sentences are fine. But several together become monotonous. Listen to what is happening. The writing is getting boring. The sound of it drones. It's like a stuck record. The ear demands some variety.
>
> Now listen. I vary the sentence length, and I create music. Music. The writing sings. It has a pleasant rhythm, a lilt, a harmony. I use short sentences. And I use sentences of medium length. And sometimes, when I am certain the reader is rested, I will engage him with a sentence of considerable length, a sentence that burns with energy and builds with all the impetus of a crescendo, the roll of the drums, the crash of the cymbals – sounds that say listen to this, it is important.[71]

Below is the opening paragraph of Ben Okri's magical realist novel *The Famished Road*, which won the Booker Prize in 1991. As you read it, notice how its rhythm changes:

> In the beginning there was a river. The river became a road and the road branched out to the whole world. And because the road was once a river it was always hungry. In that land of beginnings spirits mingled with the unborn. We could assume numerous forms. Many of us were birds. We knew no boundaries. There was much feasting, playing and sorrowing. We

71 Quoted on Aerogrammestudio.com, as quoted in Roy Peter Clark's *Writing Tools: 50 Essential Strategies for Every Writer* (2008).

> feasted much because of the beautiful terrors of eternity. We played much because we were free. And we borrowed much because there were always those amongst us who had just returned from the world of the living. They had returned inconsolable for all the love they had left behind, all the suffering they hadn't redeemed, all that they hadn't understood, and for all that they had barely begun to learn before they were drawn back to the land of origins.[72]

See how the sentences vary in length. They begin short but become longer – with the last sentence the longest, as if the narrator is finding his stride. The repetition of certain words also aids the flow:

> In the beginning there was a river. The river became a road and the road branched out to the whole world. And because the road was once a river it was always hungry.

Some sentences begin with "and" – this softens the repetition of "we" and smooths the flow, particularly between the very short opening sentences (which might otherwise give the passage a halting rhythm). For more on beginning a sentence with "and", read on.

72 Ben Okri, *The Famished Road*, p. 3.

One sentence or two?

Breaking a statement into two sentences can be a good way to emphasise a point. But it's important to strike a balance between fluency and focus, so take care to vary your sentence length to keep your reader interested.

ONE SENTENCE (FOR FLOW)	TWO SENTENCES (FOR EMPHASIS)
Despite the mining sector strengthening in the first half of 2017, production remains depressed by historical standards.	The mining sector strengthened in the first half of 2017. Nonetheless, production remains depressed.
The latest research suggests that awareness campaigns in this area may not work and could be counterproductive.	The latest research suggests that awareness campaigns in this field may not work. In fact, they may be counterproductive.
Tremendous progress has been made in improving the capacity of storage devices and commercialising newly developed technologies, but cheap long-term electricity storage is still largely out of reach or impractical.	Tremendous progress has been made in improving the capacity of storage devices and in commercialising newly developed technologies. But cheap long-term electricity storage is still largely out of reach – or impractical.

Starting a sentence with a conjunction is another good way to vary sentence flow. In the following example (in which a CEO states her company's three main ambitions), notice how the staccato repetition of "we want" is offset by the structure of the third sentence:

> We want to centralise innovation in our culture. We want to reorient our business towards excellent customer service. And we want our purpose to be clear – not just internally, but to our customers, clients, shareholders and society.

The secret to the third sentence is that it is longer than the previous two, begins with "and" rather than "we", and contains a dash that both aids flow and adds emphasis.

In school, many of us were taught not to begin a sentence with a conjunction like "but", "and" or "because". But this approach is wrong. And we're proving it to you now. Because there's nothing wrong with using these words to start a sentence.

Improving rhythm and focus with the active and passive voice

It may take a bit of time to get the feel for whether a sentence is in the active or passive voice, but it's reassuring to know that we switch between the two when we speak, even if we're not aware of it. We generally choose the active voice to describe someone or something performing an action and the passive voice for when the actor is not relevant.

It's easy to see these choices at work in fiction. As you read the following extract from Chimamanda Ngozi Adichie's novel *Half of a Yellow Sun* (2006), notice the alternation in focus between the character performing an action ("Ugwu turned off the tap ...") and general observation about the situation ("There were books ..."). Notice, too, how Adichie varies her sentence length.

> Ugwu turned off the tap, turned it on again, then off. On and off and on and off until he was laughing at the magic of the running water and the chicken and bread that lay balmy in his stomach. He went past the living room and into the corridor. There were books piled on the shelves and tables in the three bedrooms, on the sink and cabinets in the bathroom, stacked from floor to ceiling in the study, and in the store, old journals were stacked next to crates of Coke and cartons of Premier beer. Some of the books were placed face down, open, as though Master had not yet finished reading them but had hastily gone on to another. Ugwu tried to read the titles, but most were too long, too difficult. *Non-Parametric Methods. An African Survey. The Great Chain of Being. The Norman Impact Upon England.*[73]

It would be tedious if every sentence was in the active voice, beginning with "Ugwu" or "He", or if every sentence was short. The variation in voice and sentence length makes the passage more readable, with some longer sentences mimicking the character wandering through his employer's house and the short sentences at the end capturing the titles of the books he notices.

---

73 Chimamanda Ngozi Adichie, *Half of a Yellow Sun*, p. 7.

If you're writing non-fiction, the active voice will make your sentences more concise and generally more immediate. As we saw in Chapter 1, however, there are times when the passive voice is more appropriate. As in fiction, too much of one or the other voice will make your writing monotonous. To avoid that problem, try to alternate between the two, like this:

> Both samples will be tested as indicated in the technical data sheets. We will then analyse the results to determine where we can make improvements.

As indicated by the underlined phrases, the first sentence is in the passive voice and the second is in the active. We could rewrite the second sentence in the passive as "The results will be analysed" – but by using the active voice we shift the rhythm and the focus, which are important elements in making your writing easy to read.

In the following example, the sentence on the left is harder to read because the verb phrase ("executed this protocol") is separated from the agent of the action ("scientists"). In the sentence on the right, the passive voice allows us to make the object of the action ("the protocol") the focus of the sentence, with the information about the agent of the action immediately following it.

AWKWARD ACTIVE VOICE SENTENCE	MORE COMFORTABLE PASSIVE VOICE VERSION
Scientists familiar with the process but who were not directly involved in designing the project executed this protocol.	This protocol was executed by scientists familiar with the process but who were not directly involved in designing the project.

Do you notice any difference in focus in the following two sentences?

> The rapidly rising public debt poses serious risks to the economy.
> The risks posed by the rapidly rising public debt to the economy are serious.

The first sentence, which is in the active voice, is more direct and less awkward than the second, which is in the passive voice. Context will dictate whether you should be focusing on the debt or the risks.

As shown by the examples in this section, the active and passive voice should be used interchangeably and with care. Your most important consideration should be to write clearly, followed closely by ensuring that your ideas are focused and flow logically.

In non-fiction writing, however, prefer the active voice to the passive voice as your first port of call.

The evolution of language and conscious word choice

Like language itself, terminology and conscious word choice evolve. Most large organisations create style guides that are updated from time to time. They govern not only technical matters (capitalisation, acronyms, treatment of numbers, naming conventions) but also questions of identity and representation. Here's how *The Associated Press (AP) Stylebook* – the leading style guide for journalists in the United States, which is used by many other large organisations – approaches one set of identity questions:

> AP's style is now to capitalize Black in a racial, ethnic or cultural sense, conveying an essential and shared sense of history, identity and community among people who identify as Black, including those in the African diaspora and within Africa. The lowercase black is a color, not a person. AP style will continue to lowercase the term white in racial, ethnic and cultural senses ... These decisions align with long-standing capitalization of distinct racial and ethnic identifiers such as Latino, Asian American and Native American. Our discussions on style and language consider many points, including the need to be inclusive and respectful in our storytelling and the evolution of language.[74]

This is but one example. The rules of usage vary significantly between countries and regions, propelled by social change. In the United States, the civil rights movement resulted in significant linguistic changes, and recent protests against racism and police brutality have brought the question of language to the fore once again. South Africa's democratic revolution overturned not only apartheid

74 AP News, "Explaining AP style on Black and white", 20 July 2020.

laws that categorised every person in the country as "White", "Coloured" or "Bantu",[75] but a host of linked racist language practices. Within the liberation movement, proponents of black consciousness carved out a lasting connection between language and politics by referring to African, Indian and Coloured South Africans collectively as black people. Today, the use and understanding of these terms remains in flux.

Not every term that comes to the fore gains traction. The term Pan-Africanism, which arose in the waning years of the nineteenth century, is today widely accepted and forms a foundational element of the African Union. In contrast, the word "Azania", meaning "the land of the blacks", was a term that Arab traders used to describe east Africa in the first century BCE.[76] Attempts, beginning in the early 1970s, by some South African political activists to have this term widely adopted now amount to a mere historical footnote.

Further afield, consider the evolution of how people of Latin American ancestry are described in the United States. For several decades, the terms "Latino" and "Latina" (Spanish being a grammatically gendered language) have been broadly accepted. In recent years, the term "Latinx" has been proposed to describe people in a gender-inclusive manner. But it hasn't entirely caught on. As one observer noted:

> Opponents of transphobia and sexism leaven their social media posts, academic papers and workplace Slack chats with the term. Liberal politicians use it. Civil rights litigators use it. Social scientists use it. Public health experts like Anthony Fauci use it. Merriam-Webster added it to the dictionary in 2018. But the label has not won wide adoption among the 61 million people of Latin American descent living in the United States.[77]

In other words, the jury is still out. Similar considerations apply to the use of terms that have an implicit (if long overlooked) gender bias: for example, today it's common for terms like "spokesperson" and "chairperson" to be used rather than "spokesman" and "chairman". *The AP Stylebook* recommends gender-

---

75 Population Registration Act No. 30 of 1950.

76 Oxford African American Studies Center, "Azania".

77 Jose A. Del Real, "'Latinx' hasn't even caught on among Latinos. It never will.", *The Washington Post*, 18 December 2020.

neutral language when possible: for instance, using "they"/"them" rather than "she" or "he". (Bear in mind that you can also use "they", "their" or "them" as a singular pronoun if you're not sure of the gender of the person being referred to – for example, "The customer returned their purchase with a complaint.") However, *The AP Stylebook* offers the following caution: "Balance these aims with common sense, respect for the language, and an understanding that gender-neutral or gender-inclusive language is evolving and in some cases is challenging to achieve."[78]

The overriding point here is that careful writers take note of history and present trends, and consult style guides, before leaping in one or another direction with their choice of words.[79]

Dealing with sensitive issues

No one likes to hear bad news. But if you tell people that everything is fine when they know otherwise, you will lose their respect. The language that companies and individuals use to deal publicly with mistakes, disclosures or revelations that reflect badly on them can reveal their values.

If you have to convey unpleasant news or address a controversial topic, you have a few options. You could avoid mentioning the problematic issue altogether and rather focus on positive points – a bad idea! You could use euphemisms to soften the edge of your message – a slightly less bad idea that is associated with "spin". Or you could address the issue directly, providing context and explanation. It's important to find the right tone.

How to confront the facts

If an uncomfortable issue is public knowledge, it's necessary to address it. However, you can generally adopt a positive outlook that points to your efforts to repair the situation while acknowledging the reality. Below are two examples of handling difficult facts in a way that is appropriate for the audience.

78 AP Stylebook, "What's new in the AP Stylebook, 55th edition?" 23 November 2020.

79 For more discussion of gender neutrality in language, see Stephen Pinker, *The Sense of Style*, pp. 255–262.

In the extract below, taken from a major African retailer's 2019 integrated report, the chief executive discusses the facts of his company's disappointing performance. Notice how he supplements the results with reassuring, positive points (underlined) about his employees' fortitude and the company's investments in future success.

> Although this year has tested our resilience, the fundamentals of our business remain strong. We experienced difficult trading conditions in our largest markets and unanticipated internal setbacks that caused distribution bottlenecks. Our trading profit after accounting for hyperinflation declined to R6.9 billion, a drop of 14.3% on the previous year. As a result, our diluted headline earnings per share contracted 19.6%. But our sales performance in our South African business recovered in the second half of this year, proving the fortitude of our people, our brands and our operations. Our Non-RSA business endured tough conditions and reported losses this year but in our view operated stores worthy of commendation.
>
> We have invested in our future by expanding our talented management team, implementing an enterprise-wide system across the business and improving governance. We look ahead with confidence in our resources and plan to increase our resilience and profitability in the long term.[80]

In comparison, consider the first two paragraphs of the foreword to South Africa's *Budget Review* for 2018. Here again the positives are weighed up against the negatives, but the tone is more sober than in the previous example, implying that this economic reckoning will be felt by all South Africans:

> The 2018 Budget arrives at a moment of opportunity for South Africa. A renewed sense of optimism has provided a much-needed boost to confidence and investment. The economic outlook has improved. And government has expressed a new resolve to strengthen policy coordination.
>
> Yet this positive turn of events should not blind us to the enormous economic and fiscal challenges facing our country. Economic growth is far too low to reduce alarmingly high unemployment and inequality.

---

80 Shoprite Holdings Ltd, *Integrated Annual Report 2019*, p. 10.

> Revenue collection, on which government depends to fund social and economic spending programmes, will fall short of projections by R48.2 billion in 2017/18. The finances of several state-owned companies are in a precarious state.[81]

In a formal document like this – which will be widely used for making important decisions, including on investment and employment – it would not be prudent to diverge from hard facts, uncomfortable though they are.

Mind your euphemisms

Euphemisms – words or phrases used to avoid saying something unpleasant – have earned their disreputable reputation through overuse by those who seek to hide the truth.

George Orwell famously declared that "the great enemy of clear language is insincerity". In "Politics and the English Language" (1946), he wrote:

> In our time, political speech and writing are largely the defence of the indefensible. Things like the continuance of British rule in India, the Russian purges and deportations, the dropping of the atom bombs on Japan, can indeed be defended, but only by arguments which are too brutal for most people to face, and which do not square with the professed aims of political parties. Thus political language has to consist largely of euphemism, question-begging and sheer cloudy vagueness.[82]

The military, whose field of expertise is violence or "the use of force", is a rich source of euphemisms. We usually think of "enhance" as having a positive connotation, as in "an enhanced quality of life". But "enhanced interrogation techniques", a phrase popularised by the Bush administration, means torture.[83] And, of course, there is South Africa's contribution of "load shedding", which seems to suggest a lightening of one's burden, but in reality means that the lights go out.

---

81 National Treasury, Republic of South Africa, 2018 *Budget Review*, Foreword, p. vii.

82 George Orwell, "Politics and the English language."

83 See William J. Astore's article "All the euphemisms we use for 'war'", *The Nation*, 15 April 2016.

The thoughtless euphemism immediately raises hackles. Take the example of United Airlines. In April 2017, passenger David Dao was forcibly removed from an overbooked plane for refusing to give up his seat at the management's request. The scuffle was filmed on a mobile phone and went viral. The CEO of United Airlines, Oscar Munoz, said, "This is an upsetting event to all of us here at United. I apologize for having to re-accommodate these customers." Poor choice of words: it was not nearly as upsetting to United as it was to the passenger, and "re-accommodate" fails to acknowledge that the passenger was manhandled and sustained a bloody nose. The apology lacks sincerity and sensitivity. Munoz subsequently had to issue a new apology and settle up with the passenger.

Be open and honest

A better example of a public apology is a tweet by the 2018 Nobel prize winner in chemistry, Dr Frances Arnold. She was apologising for having to retract an academic paper for publication because of missing data and the results of her study not being reproducible:

> For my first work-related tweet of 2020, I am totally bummed to announce that we have retracted last year's paper on enzymatic synthesis of beta-lactams. The work has not been reproducible. ... It is painful to admit, but important to do so. I apologize to all. I was a bit busy when this was submitted, and did not do my job well.[84]

The apology shows humility, which is more likely to secure the respect of her peers and the public than an attempt to excuse herself.

Reputation matters. Often it hinges on the words one chooses for dealing with a difficult matter. Airbnb CEO Brian Chesky's letter announcing the company's new anti-discrimination policy is an example of honest acknowledgement of problems. What stands out is Chesky's personal tone (his use of "we", "our" and "I"). He takes personal responsibility for his company's slow response to the issue and links a social problem directly to his business mission.

> At the heart of our mission is the idea that people are fundamentally good

84 Poppy Noor, "Nobel prize winner demonstrates the best way to apologize", *The Guardian*, 6 January 2020.

> and every community is a place where you can belong. ... Discrimination is the opposite of belonging, and its existence on our platform jeopardizes this core mission. Bias and discrimination have no place on Airbnb, and we have zero tolerance for them. Unfortunately, we have been slow to address these problems, and for this I am sorry. I take responsibility for any pain or frustration this has caused members of our community. We will not only make this right; we will work to set an example that other companies can follow.[85]

Find the right tone

We all occasionally need to deal with sensitive issues. Smooth professional relations depend on finding the right words to inform someone politely that you're not happy with something.

Perhaps a colleague always arrives late for meetings, talks too loudly in the office or has some other objectionable behaviour. How do you let them know that they need to show more consideration for others? You don't want to convey the impression that the issue is personal, nor do you want to be vague, hesitant or apologetic. You need to find a way to express your feelings firmly but politely – with the consideration you'd like them to demonstrate towards yourself and others.

Sometimes it's better to speak to them in person about the issue. On the other hand, email allows you more time to compose your thoughts. Here are a couple of examples of how you could phrase your message.

85 Alex Fitzpatrick, "Airbnb CEO: 'Bias and discrimination have no place' here", *Time*, September 2016.

On office security	Hello everyone, This morning when I came into the office, I noticed that two of the windows facing the parking area were open. Office equipment can be expensive to replace, so please can we all take a renewed personal interest in office security? If you open one of the windows, please close it before you leave the office for the day. Thanks!
On being late	Hi Christo, I know traffic can be a nightmare getting to work in the mornings. But it's important that we all make an effort to get here on Mondays and Fridays a few minutes before 8 a.m. so our team meetings can start on time. Let me know if this is something you'd like to discuss.

Dealing with sensitive issues is not easy. The challenge is to find the right tone so your message doesn't sound stilted or rude. You want to be clear and considerate, assigning responsibility where necessary and speaking to the point, while inviting discussion if needed. Most of all, you want to show integrity so that your audience understands your message while appreciating how you conveyed it. An important ingredient of integrity is referring to particulars using concrete language.

To wrap up

As we've seen in this chapter, a narrative framework or well-placed image or example can help make complex or detailed information more accessible, while stylistic variation is important for keeping the reader interested. Look for opportunities to apply these approaches in your writing. Sometimes they won't be appropriate, and that's fine. The broader point here is to be aware of the range of strategies you can draw on to connect with and move your reader.

CHAPTER 6
Words in action

This chapter focuses on four modes of communication where the tips and techniques discussed earlier can be applied to great effect: speeches, opinion pieces, summaries and presentations. You might not have occasion to write an opinion piece or deliver a speech, but the approaches discussed here are worth knowing, and they can be rewardingly applied to other kinds of writing too.

Speeches

Many of us find it scary to stand up and speak in front of people. But facing the blank page can also be intimidating. For Trevor Noah, host of *The Daily Show* and author of the memoir *Born a Crime* (2016), what scares him most about writing is "not having an audience in front of me":

> Onstage, I tell a joke or a story and I know right away if it's working or not. I know how to handle that. With a book, you're writing hundreds of pages and putting them out in the world and you don't know what the response will be until the reviews come back.[86]

Noah's comment highlights an important difference between speaking and writing. When you speak, your audience is physically present. They can understand the immediate context, observe your facial expressions and body language, and hear the tone, volume and pace of your voice. Equally, the audience's body language (showing interest, boredom, scepticism or some other attitude) may affect your delivery. Writing doesn't allow this kind of interaction, which is why it's so important to choose your words carefully and gauge the effect they're likely to have on your reader.

In speeches you need to use words to signpost your intentions, because the audience is listening "blind" and doesn't have the benefit of being able to

86 Trevor Noah, "Powell's Q&A: Trevor Noah, author of *Born a Crime*", PowellsBooks.Blog, 14 November 2016.

skim forward or check the text. Effective public speaking requires deft use of rhetorical devices to capture an audience's attention and ensure they remember your main points.

In writing a speech, remember three things: tell a story, make it relevant and don't go on too long. This is the advice of Lewis Pugh, a much-in-demand motivational speaker famous for completing long-distance swims in every ocean, including the Arctic, wearing just a Speedo:

> The more talks I did, the more I realised that CEOs and business leaders are, with respect, just the same as kids in a township seminary or a Cape Flats school. They are easily distracted. They are busy and under pressure, so you've got to go in there and grab them, and tell them a story. ... And more importantly, make sure you have finished talking before they have finished listening! Keep it short. Keep it tight. No waffle. I had to take the stories of the Antarctic and the North Pole and make them meaningful and relevant to their businesses and their lives.[87]

We've been here before: consider your audience!

What makes a good speech?

A powerful address means more than reading a text out loud: it needs to be incisive, sincere and inspiring. It needs to be evidence-based and have rhythm. Most importantly, the speaker needs to form a strong connection with the audience. Below are a few tips for constructing a compelling speech.

Begin your speech with an icebreaker or welcome – some way of hooking the audience's interest. One way to do this is to tell a story that is brief, relevant and stimulating.[88] Another is to pose a thought-provoking question. Or you could present a striking statistic and point to the consequences of this in years to come. A quotation could also work, but use them sparingly: the audience is there to listen to you, not to hear you recite what others have said. Using the pronouns "I", "you" and "we" will help make the audience feel like they're part of a conversation.

---

87 Lewis Pugh, *21 Yaks and a Speedo*, pp. 213–214.

88 William Safire, *Lend Me Your Ears: Great Speeches in History*, p. 23.

A good speech needs purpose and focus. What is the occasion? What unique perspective will the speech offer? At the outset, outline the key points you're going to cover. As you move through your material, remind your audience what you've covered and what you'll be focusing on next: you need to actively bring your listeners along with you. Towards the end, recap the key points and reflect on what you've said. In other words: say what you're going to say; say it; then say what you've said.[89]

Here's how Steve Jobs, the then-CEO of Apple, opened his commencement address at Stanford University on 12 June 2005:

> I am honored to be with you today at your commencement from one of the finest universities in the world. I never graduated from college. Truth be told, this is the closest I've ever gotten to a college graduation. Today I want to tell you three stories from my life. That's it. No big deal. Just three stories.
>
> The first story is about connecting the dots.[90]

Jobs goes on to describe how, looking back, he can see coherence in the choices he made throughout his adult life, even if he didn't recognise that coherence at the time. He introduces the remaining two parts of his speech with a simple sentence each: "my second story is about love and loss"; "my third story is about death". In keeping with the straightforward advice he offers his audience of graduates, Jobs uses clear language and simple sentences. Here's a sample:

> I'm pretty sure none of this would have happened if I hadn't been fired from Apple. It was awful-tasting medicine, but I guess the patient needed it. Sometimes life hits you in the head with a brick. Don't lose faith. I'm convinced that the only thing that kept me going was that I loved what I did.

Rhythm and vivid images can also help to convey your message effectively. One way to generate rhythm is through repetition of words and phrases. Clusters of three help to drive a message home and make it easier for listeners to recall

---

89 William Safire, *Lend me Your Ears*, p. 31.

90 Steve Jobs, "'You've got to find what you love,' Jobs says", *Stanford News*, 14 June 2005.

key points. Reversal is another useful rhetorical strategy (for example, John F. Kennedy's famous "Ask not what your country can do for you, but what you can do for your country").

Strong linking words are essential for giving a speech cohesion – they are the equivalent of hand gestures: now, so, therefore, in light of this, even though, however, but, although. Questions are also an effective way of engaging the audience's attention. Long paragraphs filled with jargon, statements of fact and quotations are deadly – they will put your audience to sleep. Don't just tell: show your ideas by using images, whether that involves describing a concrete situation or using a metaphor. Images are easier for the audience to grasp than theoretical and discursive language.

As an illustration of some of these points, consider the opening lines of Barack Obama's 2008 election victory speech (note in particular the phrases we've highlighted in bold):

> If there is anyone out there **who still** doubts that America is a place where all things are possible; **who still** wonders if the dream of our founders is alive in our time; **who still** questions the power of our democracy, tonight is your answer.
>
> **It's the answer** told by **lines that stretched around schools and churches** in numbers this nation has never seen; by people who waited three hours and four hours, many for the very first time in their lives, because they believed that this time must be different; that their voice could be that difference.
>
> **It's the answer** spoken by **young and old**, **rich and poor**, **Democrat and Republican**, black, white, Latino, Asian, Native American, gay, straight, disabled and not disabled – Americans who sent a message to the world that we have never been a collection of **red states and blue states**; we are, and always will be, the United States of America.
>
> **It's the answer** that led those who have been told for so long by so many to be cynical, and fearful, and doubtful of what we can achieve to put their hands on the arc of history and bend it once more toward the hope of a better day.

> It's been a long time coming, but tonight, because of what we did on this day, in this election, at this defining moment, change has come to America.[91]

Note how he repeats phrases to create rhythm: "If there is anyone who still ..., who still ..., who still ..."; "It's the answer told ... It's the answer spoken ... It's the answer that led ...". He uses binaries ("young and old, rich and poor ...") to suggest opposites that have been reconciled. And he provides images of concrete things that carry a symbolic meaning: "lines that stretched around schools and churches"; "red states and blue states".

Soaring rhetoric, rhythm and counterpoint are consistent features of Obama's speeches. But a speech doesn't have to make such bold flourishes to be moving. Here's an example of a powerful speech that uses ordinary language, taken from Malala Yousafzai's address at the United Nations Youth Assembly on her sixteenth birthday in 2013:

> Dear brothers and sisters, do remember one thing: Malala Day is not my day. Today is the day of every woman, every boy and every girl who have raised their voice for their rights.
>
> There are hundreds of human rights activists and social workers who are not only speaking for their rights, but who are struggling to achieve their goal of peace, education and equality. Thousands of people have been killed by the terrorists and millions have been injured. I am just one of them. So here I stand. So here I stand, one girl, among many. I speak not for myself, but so those without a voice can be heard.[92]

Her sentences are simple but powerful, as is the image of being one girl among many.

The following extract is from the speech Nelson Mandela gave at his inauguration as president of South Africa on 10 May 1994. Look at how he emphasises his vision of national unity by speaking of "we", how he describes South Africans' patriotism in terms of physical aspects of the landscape and how he compares

---

91 Barack Obama, "Transcript of Barack Obama's victory speech", NPR, 5 November 2008.

92 Malala Yousafzai, "Malala Yousafzai: 'Our books and our pens are the most powerful weapons'", *The Guardian*, 12 July 2013.

the changing mood in the country to the changing seasons. These images make it easier for his listeners to share in his vision.

> To my compatriots, I have no hesitation in saying that each one of us is as intimately attached to the soil of this beautiful country as are the famous jacaranda trees of Pretoria and the mimosa trees of the bushveld.
>
> Each time one of us touches the soil of this land, we feel a sense of personal renewal. The national mood changes as the seasons change.
>
> We are moved by a sense of joy and exhilaration when the grass turns green and the flowers bloom.
>
> That spiritual and physical oneness we all share with this common homeland explains the depth of the pain we all carried in our hearts as we saw our country tear itself apart in a terrible conflict, and as we saw it spurned, outlawed and isolated by the peoples of the world, precisely because it has become the universal base of the pernicious ideology and practice of racism and racial oppression.
>
> We, the people of South Africa, feel fulfilled that humanity has taken us back into its bosom, that we, who were outlaws not so long ago, have today been given the rare privilege to be host to the nations of the world on our own soil.[93]

It is not just the lyricism of Mandela's words that is rousing (for example, "when the grass turns green and the flowers bloom") but his repetition of the word "we", which is warmly inclusive and rebuts the idea of a segregated political system. While his elevated tone is appropriate for the historic occasion, his goal is to speak to individual South Africans.

Finally, a good speech needs to end memorably. It shouldn't end abruptly or peter out. Let your audience know that you're approaching the conclusion. Emphasise the most important messages. Then leave them with a rousing last line – it might be a vote of appreciation, a motivating message, a call to action or an amusing reflection or choice of words.

---

93 Nelson Mandela, "Nelson Mandela at his inauguration as president of South Africa, Pretoria", speech transcript, 10 May 1994.

Below is the second half of Bob Dylan's acceptance speech on winning the Nobel Prize in Literature in 2016. He didn't attend the ceremony because of "prior commitments" (he was gigging in Las Vegas), so instead he wrote a speech to be read out in his absence. It's a good example to end with because it reflects on how it doesn't matter so much whether something was written to be spoken or read. What matters is whether the message resonates with the audience, whether it speaks to them in the broadest sense.

The Nobel Prize is a prestigious award, but Dylan does not puff up his language to suit the dignified occasion. Instead, his voice remains direct and unpretentious, his musings conversational and accessible to the common person. In tone, his words are respectful and gracious but also self-deprecating. He compares himself to Shakespeare only to highlight the kind of mundane specifics that artists spend so much time focusing on.

> I was out on the road when I received this surprising news, and it took me more than a few minutes to properly process it. I began to think about William Shakespeare, the great literary figure. I would reckon he thought of himself as a dramatist. The thought that he was writing literature couldn't have entered his head. His words were written for the stage. Meant to be spoken not read. When he was writing *Hamlet*, I'm sure he was thinking about a lot of different things: "Who're the right actors for these roles?" "How should this be staged?" "Do I really want to set this in Denmark?" His creative vision and ambitions were no doubt at the forefront of his mind, but there were also more mundane matters to consider and deal with. "Is the financing in place?" "Are there enough good seats for my patrons?" "Where am I going to get a human skull?" I would bet that the farthest thing from Shakespeare's mind was the question "Is this *literature*?"
>
> When I started writing songs as a teenager, and even as I started to achieve some renown for my abilities, my aspirations for these songs only went so far. I thought they could be heard in coffee houses or bars, maybe later in places like Carnegie Hall, the London Palladium. If I was really dreaming big, maybe I could imagine getting to make a record and then hearing my songs on the radio. That was really the big prize in my mind.

> Making records and hearing your songs on the radio meant that you were reaching a big audience and that you might get to keep doing what you had set out to do.
>
> Well, I've been doing what I set out to do for a long time, now. I've made dozens of records and played thousands of concerts all around the world. But it's my songs that are at the vital center of almost everything I do. They seemed to have found a place in the lives of many people throughout many different cultures and I'm grateful for that.
>
> But there's one thing I must say. As a performer I've played for 50,000 people and I've played for 50 people and I can tell you that it is harder to play for 50 people. 50,000 people have a singular persona, not so with 50. Each person has an individual, separate identity, a world unto themselves. They can perceive things more clearly. Your honesty and how it relates to the depth of your talent is tried. The fact that the Nobel committee is so small is not lost on me.
>
> But, like Shakespeare, I too am often occupied with the pursuit of my creative endeavors and dealing with all aspects of life's mundane matters. "Who are the best musicians for these songs?" "Am I recording in the right studio?" "Is this song in the right key?" Some things never change, even in 400 years.
>
> Not once have I ever had the time to ask myself, "Are my songs *literature*?"
>
> So, I do thank the Swedish Academy, both for taking the time to consider that very question, and, ultimately, for providing such a wonderful answer.[94]

There are many ways to start and end a speech: whichever way you choose, your speech should leave the audience feeling invigorated, feeling that the world is fresh with possibility.

94 Bob Dylan, "Nobel Prize banquet speech", 10 December 2016.

Opinion pieces

We all have opinions, some of them strongly held. But to be effective, an opinion piece needs to offer clear, persuasive perspectives supported by relevant evidence. To engage and persuade your reader, your tone should be confident and direct. Given that the audience will likely be broad, it's important to avoid jargon, provide sufficient context and ensure your writing is accessible. It may be appropriate to use first-person pronouns and personal anecdotes, since the piece is based on opinion.

Many of the guidelines for speechwriting also apply here. Engage the audience through a concise introduction, which presents a main idea. The rest of the piece should persuade the reader using an argument that flows logically and cites relevant evidence. Ensure that your views are accurate and balanced.

If you're writing as a representative of an organisation, bear in mind that – unless stated otherwise – your piece will be interpreted as your organisation's official view, so make sure you don't contradict any organisational policies or public statements. If you're targeting a specific publication, check whether it offers any guidelines for an opinion piece.

Below is an extract from an opinion piece on climate change communications, written in 2018 for the journal *Civil Engineering* by one of our directors at Clarity Global. The pun and question of the title are designed to capture the reader's attention, while the subheading provides a thumbnail sketch of the problem addressed by the piece and the solution in the form of five key points. The use of questions and accessible language makes the writer's points easy to relate to, while the audience is clearly addressed as "you", a civil engineering professional. Note, though, that you don't need to be an engineer to understand the argument.

> **Communicating climate change: A hot topic?**
> Climate change presents all kinds of communication difficulties. Too often, the key message can be confused or lost because of intrinsic scientific uncertainties. This article discusses five key points to shape effective climate change communication.

When you talk to someone who isn't an Earth scientist about climate change, you're likely to get one of two responses: flat-eyed indifference – boredom, even – or panic. People tend to view climate change either as a problem that belongs to someone else, somewhere else, in some distant time, or as something too enormous to fathom, possibly coupled with a sense of helplessness at ever doing anything to address it.

Why the difference in reactions? Our communications company believes it is because of the way the scientific community works. Science is meant to be an evidence-based pursuit, with any claim to knowledge or "truth" stemming from repeated observations of the world both within the laboratory and outside it. These observations are couched in statistical methods and phrases: a good scientist will never say "X causes Y". He or she will rather describe a "strong correlation" between X and Y, and hedge their bets with a "confidence level". To confuse matters even further, climatologists rely on scientific modelling – observing the world's weather patterns over time, deriving rules from these observations and then constructing a model that allows them to predict what will happen to variable X if there are changes in variables Y and Z.

All of this serves to add complexity and uncertainty to climate change theories and forecasts. These are good scientific practices, and important requirements for furthering our understanding of the world and everything in it, but they don't make for good communication. Humans are simple creatures, capable of absorbing only small chunks of information at a given time: according to Miller's law, we can only hold between five and nine items in our working memory. All this considered, it is a terrible waste of mental bandwidth to use one of those knowledge points to convey uncertainty.

As a civil engineering professional, you play an important role in the fight against climate change. You shape the way we interact with our natural environment, whether by improving public transport systems or by building structures that reduce our energy and water usage. This means that, at times, you may be called on to communicate the importance of climate change to those who don't really know about it (or, worse, don't

> really care). We believe that playing to the narrower end of the attention spectrum and limiting your message to a maximum of five key points will help you in this endeavour. In that spirit we would like to highlight a few salient points when it comes to communicating about climate change.[95]

Here's a second example that takes up a heated issue. These are extracts from a column by Clarity Global co-founder Palesa Morudu, writing in *Business Day* in 2018, on the public debate over Winnie Mandela's legacy:

> *Part of my Soul Went with Him* is the title of a 1985 book by the woman born Nomzamo Winifred Zanyiwe Madikizela. As South Africa pays tribute to one of its remarkable daughters, who will be buried on Saturday, it is fitting to ask what part of our "soul" as a nation has gone with Winnie Madikizela Mandela.
>
> This period of national mourning has been as South African as it gets. Adherents to the politics of adulation have been in close combat with those who avow the politics of condemnation. Some praise "Winnie" because she was a fearless fighter for justice and a feminist icon; others excoriate her because she was a violent egomaniac. Hagiography meets *swart gevaar*. The contest has been shrill and depressing in equal measure, especially in the hyperventilation chamber that is Twitter.
>
> We do history a disservice if we omit the truth about the characters and events that shaped democratic South Africa. So, we must accept that Winnie Mandela was both a heroine and a villain.
>
> My very first struggle song was about Winnie Mandela. As little children playing in the dusty streets of Mamelodi, we sang that Winnie was arrested and tortured because she was fighting for our land. The apartheid government had silenced nearly everyone, mostly men, by sending them to jail and forcing them into exile.
>
> But they did not silence Winnie – a courageous and defiant black woman who stared down the brutal racist regime and declared that freedom would happen in her lifetime. She took on the mantle of "mother of the nation", for which she paid with torture, banishment and loneliness.

---

95 Shaista Amod, "Communicating climate change: A hot topic?" *Civil Engineering* 26.7 (August 2018): 21–23.

> In these conditions, the other Winnie was born. [...]
>
> The problem with portraying individuals who made a contribution as "struggle royalty" and lavishing them with such praise is that they begin to believe it. And like all royalty, they end up acting as if they are the law, and the peasants be damned.[96]

The author's argument is easy to follow because it's woven into a personal story about reconciling conflicting versions of a public figure's significance. Morudu begins by posing a question about Winnie's legacy using the title of her book about her husband. After pointing out the inadequacy of assessments that are wholly positive or negative, Morudu goes on to evoke her childhood and the singing of struggle songs that celebrated Winnie's resistance in a context of black voices being silenced. This early idealising moment is then balanced with a later impression of Winnie betraying her humble beginnings. The paragraphing helps to advance the argument by marking shifts in the context of discussion.

This example shows that narrative can be useful for developing an argument and presenting a personal point of view without making the narrative entirely personal or the piece stridently argumentative. A strong opinion does not make a strong opinion piece: more is needed. The author's point of view needs to be presented persuasively.

Summaries

Summarising is an essential skill. It's what you do when someone you've just met asks "What work do you do?" or when you tell a friend that you saw an interesting film and they say "What's it about?" A book review and the blurb on a book's back cover are also summaries of a kind. Both should give you an impression of the story, but the purpose of a blurb is to make you want to buy the book, while a review offers an assessment of quality. Titles and subtitles also serve to summarise key content, regardless of whether you're writing an essay, report, blog, book or some other kind of piece.

---

96 Palesa Morudu, "Has truth become a casualty of Winnie's rejection of accountability?" *Business Day*, 13 April 2018.

Summaries are often used to highlight the key findings of a longer, detailed document. This is particularly important for reports commissioned by large international organisations where the topic will interest a global audience.

Summaries go by different names in different kinds of publication. Documents of more than 50 pages are sometimes accompanied by an **executive summary** or **overview**. Such summaries are generally between half a page and a few pages in length, providing a snapshot of the main points. This is useful for anyone who's interested in the topic but doesn't have the time to read the full document. Similarly, the **abstract** at the beginning of an academic paper or thesis notes key findings and why they matter.

A summary is best written after the document has been completed and should accurately reflect high-level elements of the main body of the report. It usually outlines the argument, context and parameters of discussion, the research approach, key messages, and proposals or recommendations. It should be understandable by a reader who is not familiar with the intricacies of the topic under discussion. This is particularly important if the findings will be used as the basis for a decision by various readers. These readers may have good general knowledge on a topic but might not be familiar with details and so would appreciate some explanation of technical terms and issues.

Here's an example of a summary of the WWF-SA report *A Practical Guide for Community-Run Nurseries: Growing Indigenous Plants for Restoration* (2019):

> A major threat to many rivers and strategic water source areas is the ever-growing threat of water-thirsty alien invasive plants. They spread quickly, often crowding out the indigenous vegetation. Once these alien-infested areas have been cleared, they need to be maintained – and ultimately restored to a natural state, with naturally occurring plants. To this end, there is a need to propagate locally found indigenous plants that can be actively replanted back into cleared sites.
>
> Restoration not only stops further degradation of land and water resources, it also creates opportunities for those living in the water source areas to have a sustainable livelihood. Available in both English and Afrikaans, this practical "how to" guide provides an overview of the skills

> and knowledge needed to run a community-based nursery and to grow indigenous plants that can be planted back into nature. It is organised into three easy sections: introduction, general principles of propagation and propagation techniques.[97]

This summary provides useful context, highlights the key practice of restoration, and outlines the document's structure and purpose. This information should be sufficient for a reader to decide whether to read further.

Now, consider this summary of a book titled *Civilising Grass: The Art of the Lawn on the South African Highveld* (2019):

> What does the lawn want? To be watered, fertilised, mowed, admired, fretted over, ignored? This unusual question serves as a starting point for *Civilising Grass: The Art of the Lawn on the South African Highveld*, an unexpected and often disconcerting critique of one of the most common and familiar landscapes in South Africa. The lawn, Jonathan Cane argues, is not quite as innocent as we might think. Besides the fact that lawns suck up scarce water, consume chemicals, displace indigenous plants and reduce biodiversity, they are also part of a colonial lineage of dispossession and violence. They reduce the political problem of land to the aesthetic question of landscape, thereby obscuring issues of ownership, redress, belonging and labour. ...
>
> *Civilising Grass* offers a detailed reading of artistic, literary and architectural lawns between 1886 and 2017. The eclectic archive includes plans, poems, maps, gardening blogs, adverts, ethnographies and ephemera, as well as literature by Koos Prinsloo, Marlene van Niekerk and Ivan Vladislavić. In addition, the book includes colour reproductions of lawn artworks by David Goldblatt, Lungiswa Gqunta, Pieter Hugo, Anton Kannemeyer, Sabelo Mlangeni, Moses Tladi and Kemang Wa Lehulere. ...
>
> Drawing on theory and conceptual tools from interdisciplinary fields such as ecocriticism, queer theory, art history and postcolonial studies, *Civilising Grass* offers the first sustained investigation of the lawn in

---

97 Summary text and full report available at: https://www.wwf.org.za/our_research/publications/?29601/a-practical-guide-for-community-run-nurseries.

> Africa and contributes to the growing conversation about the complex relationships between humans and non-humans on the continent.[98]

This is what we get if we break down this passage into its elements:

- The questions the book explores and why they are worth exploring.
- Detail on the book's approach, contents and unique features.
- The significance of the book's findings in relation to other fields and topics of study.

This overview doesn't just inform the reader of what the book covers, it also highlights the book's significance and poses interesting questions that could persuade a reader to invest the time in reading it.

The other important function of a summary is to aid online searches. It allows people working in your field of study or on a related topic to search for a key term, browse your summary and see whether it contains material relevant to their work. In other words, a summary can serve as a marketing tool, attracting readers to your work and showing them how you are contributing to a broader conversation.

Presentations

Presentation slides are a striking visual medium for sharing information. But some common mistakes often doom a presentation:

- **DEATH BY CONTENT** – Clutter is the bane of PowerPoint, Keynote and their siblings. Overwhelming your audience with information – whether it's dense text or complex, data-heavy graphics – will ensure that almost no one will follow your presentation.
- **READING YOUR SLIDES ALOUD** – Remember, in most cases your audience can read. Don't bore them to tears by repeating what they can see on-screen.
- **RELIANCE ON GIMMICKS** – Excessive use of gimmicky animations is off-putting and can be a sign that you don't have much to say.

98 This book summary was accessed on 17 November 2021 on the Wits University Press website: https://witspress.co.za/catalogue/civilising-grass/.

A good presentation is one where the presenter speaks engagingly about crisp, relevant slide content. Pictures and graphics should complement text. Each slide should be understandable on its own, with little or no explanation by the speaker. Most importantly, the key points should be clear.

You don't need to use full sentences on a slide. Ensuring each slide has a focused heading helps to develop your argument or link discussion points across the presentation. It's not possible to do this if a slide is a data dump – a clutter of graphs, tables, text and infographics. Rather than squeezing paragraphs of text onto a slide, use keywords, boldface and bullets to highlight the most important points.

Avoid putting your speaking notes in the slide headings. You need to find a way of speaking to what's shown on the slide without repeating it. In the two examples below, the first is too long and the second is full of jargon. Keep it clear and concise.

CLUTTERED SLIDE HEADING	REVISED VERSION
Thinking through the impact of the investment rating downgrade – hypothetical responses from a general equilibrium model	Potential effects of the investment rating downgrade
Targeted interventions and remedial actions mobilised to mitigate emerging thematic risks	Emerging risks are being addressed

Developing speaking notes is a useful thinking exercise, helping you formulate what you want to say in your presentation. These notes should supplement the information shown on a slide. Avoid simply cutting and pasting a block of text from a longer source document. Rather use the notes to highlight aspects of the slides or provide useful contextual information (like background information, a definition or an explanation).

Questions are a good way to engage your audience's attention and move between points. Occasionally, you can make the heading of your slide a question to frame the content in an interesting way. But avoid the approach in Example 1: the second paragraph should not be on the slide at all and the first paragraph would work better either as a standalone slide or, trimmed, as a heading on a slide that provides a crisp set of answers.

As you draft your speaking notes and decide what information to include in your slides, repeatedly ask yourself: "What is the broader significance of this detail and how does it fit in?" This will help you create links between slides, which you can then build into your headings. To test the coherence of your presentation, copy and paste the slide headings into a Word document and check that they progress logically. For longer presentations, consider opening with a slide that provides an overview of the presentation and its purpose, and close with a summary of key points or next steps.

Example 1

How can you increase your productivity when working from home?

Let's take a look at some of the common challenges of working remotely and some simple approaches you can adopt to boost your energy, increase your focus, and ensure you work more effectively and efficiently.

Slide design is an important consideration – after all, the presentation of your ideas is achieved as much by the composition of content on the slide as the contextualising words spoken by the presenter. There's a place for minimalist slide design where the main feature is words on a blank background. But a presentation slide – like the human voice – is a versatile medium, so spend some time exploring the functionality of PowerPoint or Keynote (or an alternative programme you might be using).

We're confident you'll agree that there's not much to get excited about in the skeleton slide shown in Example 2, which is about our company's services.

But some design treatment transforms this slide. One way of visualising and vitalising this content is to add some colour, framing lines and icons, as shown in Example 3 below. Notice how the content is balanced with the symmetrical lines into an upper and lower panel, with the heading at top left counterpointed by the company icon at bottom right.

Example 2

SPECIALIST SERVICES

- Strategic communications campaigns
- Content creation and design
- Substantive editing and copy editing
- Speechwriting
- Data visualisation
- Training in clear communication

Example 3

This is a straightforward example where there's only a single focus and a few content elements. More careful composition is called for when more content, with different emphases, needs to be accommodated. The slide in Example 4 provides a detailed snapshot of an area of work in which Clarity Global specialises.

Again, balance is a crucial element for focusing the viewer's eye, with various colours framing the column of text. The dual focus on the featured clients is achieved through different colours but consistent format: red lighting up the subheading "Client spotlight", black text distinguishing the client names and contextual detail, and the grey bullets providing a key point about the client and a key point about the work we've done for them. Finally, the client icons to the right counterbalance the report cover to the left. Of course, the cover image brings an appealing warmth to the whole slide.

Example 4

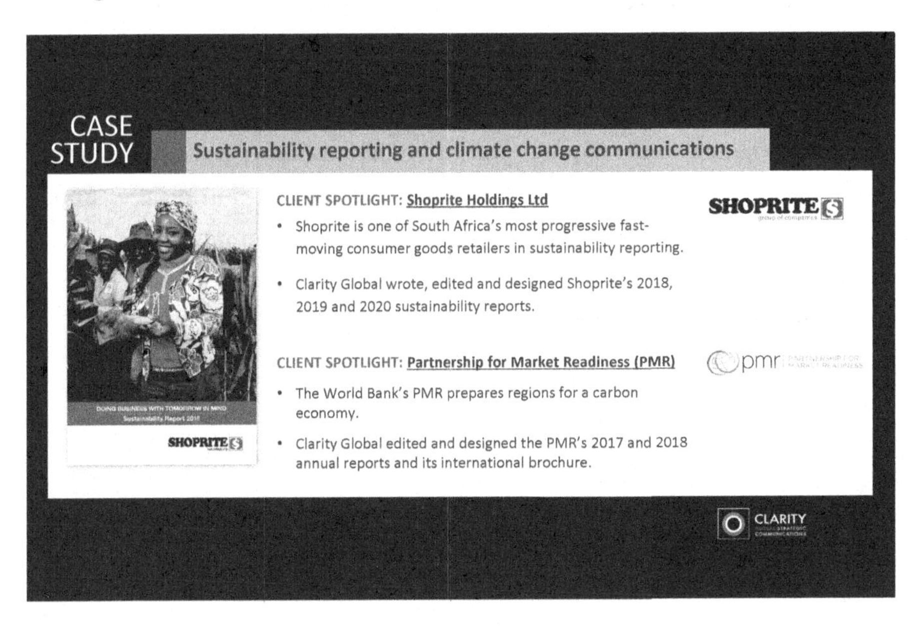

Behind this slide lie many choices, conversations, trials, errors and adjustments: from the topic of the slide, through the choice of words and clients, to all the elements of design (spacing, font size and colour, layout, etc.). And this, remember, is just a static outtake from what in reality might be a dynamic, live presentation by a member of our team.

The design and content of your slides make up only half of your presentation: the other, more important half is how you bring your content to life in your delivery (some would say delivery counts for most of a presentation's effectiveness, just as your body language and tone account for much of how someone interprets the words you speak).

To wrap up

The ability to write clearly and concisely is valuable at all times, but particularly when constraints of time or space are imposed by the form of your communication. The audience of a speech or presentation, and the reader of an opinion piece or summary, will greatly appreciate ideas condensed into easily accessible form – and will notice when they are not.

Today, oceans of content are at our fingertips and reading habits are shifting as communication technologies evolve. How much of what you read grips you? How much of it widens your view and deepens your understanding of the world? How much of it moves you to recommend it to others?

Becoming a better writer requires you to become more conscious of yourself as a reader. Empowered with that fuller awareness, you'll find it easier to put into practice – again and again, in a spirit of gradual improvement – what you've learnt here about how to make your writing, in all formats, readable and meaningful to those who read it.

ACKNOWLEDGEMENTS

The authors would like to thank Darryl Accone, Dorothy Dyer, Pippa Green and Sicelo Kula for their contributions to discussion in the formative stages of this book. Thanks also to Michalsons Attorneys for assistance with plain language and the law. At Clarity Global, Jennifer Stastny provided valuable input on the structure of the book, Lara Godwin and Raykie Martin made the content shipshape with their sharp-eyed edits, Shaista Amod helped craft the discussion of data design, and Natasha Ndlebe helped compile the index. We extend our thanks to Charity Agasaro, Dorothy Dyer, Pippa Green, Ferial Haffajee, Glynis Lloyd and Dumisani Kewuti for their reader comments and insights. Special thanks to Georgia Demertzis for her skilful design of the book and Sandra Dodson for ensuring a smooth production process. We also thank Cover2Cover Books for coming on board as a publishing partner.

In thinking about what makes a better writer, we benefited from the work done by many others – in particular, William Strunk, Jr, and E.B. White's classic *The Elements of Style*, William Zinsser's *On Writing Well* and Benjamin Dreyer's astute and amusing *Dreyer's English: An Utterly Correct Guide to Clarity and Style.* And finally, we would like to thank the thousands of participants in Clarity Global training courses, hailing from many countries, whose questions, contributions and real-world insights have helped to shape this modest volume.

INDEX

BIBLIOGRAPHY

Achebe, Chinua. *Things Fall Apart*. London: William Heinemann, 1958.

Adichie, Chimamanda Ngozi. *Half of a Yellow Sun*. New York: Anchor Books, 2007.

Amod, Shaista. "Communicating climate change: A hot topic?" *Civil Engineering* 26.7 (August 2018): 21–23.

Angelou, Maya. Interviewed by George Plimpton. The Art of Fiction No. 119. *The Paris Review* 116 (Fall 1990). New York: Paris Review Inc.

Astore, William J. "All the euphemisms we use for 'war.'" *The Nation*, 15 April 2016.

AP News. "Explaining AP style on Black and white." 20 July 2020. Available at: https://apnews.com/article/9105661462.

AP Stylebook. "What's new in the AP Stylebook, 55th edition?" 23 November 2020. Available at: https://www.apstylebook.com/help?query=gender+neutral.

Baker, Nicholson. *The Everlasting Story of Nory*. New York: Vintage, 1998.

Baxter, Roger. "Crucial for SA to focus on leadership compact to effect structural reform." *Business Day*, 3 June 2020.

Buffett, Warren. Chairman's letter. Berkshire Hathaway Annual Report 2000. 3–21. Available at: https://www.berkshirehathaway.com/2000ar/2000ar.pdf.

---. Preface to *A Plain English Handbook*. Washington, DC: US Securities and Exchange Commission, 1998.

Cain, Sian. "150m Shades of Grey: How the decade's runaway bestseller changed our sex lives." *The Guardian*, 15 January 2020.

Cane, Jonathan. *Civilising Grass: The Art of the Lawn on the South African Highveld*. Wits University Press, 2019.

Castle, Stephen. "Alternate Brexit plans rejected; Theresa May offers to step down." *New York Times*, 28 March 2019.

Chandra, Rishita. "Eco-anxiety: Managing mental health amid climate change impacts." *The Jakarta Post*, 3 December 2019.

Cole, Teju. *Eight Letters to a Young Writer*. 2010. Words follow me: Archive of essays by Teju Cole for NEXT newspaper. Available at: https://wordsfollowme.files.wordpress.com/2010/10/teju-cole-eight-letters-to-a-young-writer2.pdf.

Commonwealth of Australia. *Budget Strategy and Outlook*, Budget Paper No. 1, 2018–19. Available at: https://archive.budget.gov.au/2018-19/bp1/bp1.pdf.

Debating Europe. "Arguments for and against banning guns." Available at: https://www.debatingeurope.eu/focus/arguments-banning-guns/#.XyPGv36xXIU.

Del Real, Jose A. "'Latinx' hasn't even caught on among Latinos. It never will." *The Washington Post*, 18 December 2020.

Dolan, Maura. "Federal judge is fed up with verbose lawyers and their bloated briefs." *Los Angeles Times*, 4 August 2016.

Dr Seuss. *Fox in Socks*. Penguin Random House, 1965.

Dreyer, Benjamin. *Dreyer's English: An Utterly Correct Guide to Clarity and Style*. New York: Random House, 2019.

Dylan, Bob. "Nobel Prize banquet speech." 10 December 2016. Available at: https://www.nobelprize.org/prizes/literature/2016/dylan/speech/.

Fitzpatrick, Alex. "Airbnb CEO: 'Bias and discrimination have no place' here." *Time*, September 2016.

Flood, Alison. "Donald Trump Jr tries to tidy up his book Liberal Privilege's grammar." *The Guardian*, 29 July 2020.

Fraser-Moleketi, Geraldine. "Project management in the public sector." Address given at IQPC project conference, Sandton, 26 November 2003. Transcript available at: https://www.polity.org.za/article/frasermoleketi-iqpc-project-management-conference-26112003-2003-11-26.

Garber, Megan. "Writing advice from a (newly minted) Nobel winner." *The Atlantic*, 5 October 2017.

Gettleman, Jeffrey. "Money given to Kenya, since stolen, puts Nike in spotlight." *New York Times*, 5 March 2016.

Glenn, Ian. "Should President Ramaphosa fire his speechwriters?" News24, 7 June 2020.

Government of Republic of South Africa. Consumer Protection Act 68 of 2008. Pretoria.

Jobs, Steve. "'You've got to find what you love,' Jobs says." *Stanford News*, 14 June 2005.

Kansas City Star. "The Star Copy Style." Available at: https://www.kansascity.com/entertainment/books/article10632713.ece/BINARY/The%20Star%20Copy%20Style.pdf.

Kellaway, Lucy. "Corporate jargon scales new heights." *Financial Times*, 8 January 2017.

King, Stephen. *On Writing: A Memoir of the Craft*. New York: Scribner, 2000.

Language Log. "Noun pile of the week." 14 December 2016. Available at: https://languagelog.ldc.upenn.edu/nll/index.php?s=%22noun+pile%22.

Mandela, Nelson. "Nelson Mandela at his inauguration as president of South Africa, Pretoria." 10 May 1994. Speech transcript available at: http://www.mandela.gov.za/mandela_speeches/1994/940510_inauguration.htm.

Masango, Lebohang. "The importance of getting the African youth involved in promoting a culture of reading." Available at: https://nalibali.org/the-importance-of-getting-the-african-youth-involved-in-promoting-a-culture-of-reading.

Mda, Zakes. *The Zulus of New York*. Cape Town: Penguin Random House, 2000.

Moretti, Franco and Dominique Pestre. "Bankspeak: The language of World Bank reports." *New Left Review* 92 (March–April 2015): 75–99.

Morudu, Palesa. "Has truth become a casualty of Winnie's rejection of accountability?" *Business Day*, 13 April 2018.

National Aeronautics Space Administration. "What is the Ozone Hole?" Available at: https://ozonewatch.gsfc.nasa.gov/facts/hole_SH.html.

National Treasury, Republic of South Africa. 2018 *Budget Review*. Pretoria.

Nehanda Radio. "Corpse sex kill threat prisoner gets 45 year sentence." 14 December 2016. Available at: https://nehandaradio.com/2016/12/14/corpse-sex-kill- threat-prisoner-gets-45-year-sentence.

Ndebele, Njabulo. *The Cry of Winnie Mandela*. Cape Town: David Philip, 2003.

Noah, Trevor. "Powell's Q&A: Trevor Noah, author of *Born a Crime*." Powells Books Blog, 14 November 2016.

Noor, Poppy. "Nobel prize winner demonstrates the best way to apologize." *The Guardian*, 6 January 2020.

Nugent, Ciara. "Terrified of climate change? You might have eco-anxiety." *Time*, 21 November 2019.

Nunn, Gary. "Don't ditch the adverb, the emoji of writing." *The Guardian*, 29 April 2019.

Obama, Barack. "2018 Nelson Mandela Annual Lecture." 17 July 2018. Transcript available at: https://www.npr.org/2018/07/17/629862434/transcript-obamas-speech-at-the-2018-nelson-mandela-annual-lecture.

---. "Transcript of Barack Obama's victory speech." 5 November 2008. Available at: https://www.npr.org/templates/story/story.php?storyId=96624326.

Office of Investor Education and Assistance. *A Plain English Handbook: How to Create Clear SEC Documents*. Washington, DC: US Securities and Exchange Commission, 1998.

Okri, Ben. *The Famished Road*. London: Vintage, 1992.

Orwell, George. "Politics and the English language." 1946. Available at: https://www.orwellfoundation.com/the-orwell-foundation/orwell/essays-and-other-works/politics-and-the-english-language/.

Oxford African American Studies Center. "Azania." Available at: https://oxfordaasc.com/view/10.1093/acref/9780195301731.001.0001/acref- 9780195301731-e-40100.

Pickard, Victor. "Journalism's market failure is a crisis for democracy." *Harvard Business Review*, 12 March 2020.

Pinker, Steven. "Many of the alleged rules of writing are actually superstitions." *The Guardian*, 6 October 2015.

---. *The Sense of Style: The Thinking Person's Guide to Writing in the 21st Century*. London: Allen Lane, 2014.

---. "Why academics stink at writing." *The Chronicle of Higher Education*, 26 September 2014.

Pitjeng, Refilwe. "Bonang's 'From A to B' book misses writing ABCs." *Eyewitness News*, 3 August 2017.

Press Association. "Weight-loss pill hailed as 'holy grail' in fight against obesity." *The Guardian*, 27 August 2018.

Pugh, Lewis. *21 Yaks and a Speedo: How to Achieve your Impossible*. Cape Town: Jonathan Ball, 2013.

Quintal, Genevieve. "KPMG acts against three partners over Gupta leaks disclosures." *TimesLive*, 11 August 2017.

Rose, Steve. "'It's a war between technology and a donkey' – how AI is shaking up Hollywood." *The Guardian*, 16 January 2020.

Safire, William. *Lend Me Your Ears: Great Speeches in History*. Updated and expanded. New York and London: W.W. Norton, 2004.

Schwartz, Martin A. "Do you speak legalese?" *Florida Bar Journal* 91.4, April 2017.

Shoprite Holdings Ltd. *Integrated Annual Report* 2019.

Silver, Laura and Courtney Johnson. *Internet Connectivity Seen as Having Positive Impact on Life in Sub-Saharan Africa*. Pew Research Center, October 2018.

Smith, Cathy. "Revolutionary technologies will drive African prosperity – this is why." World Economic Forum, 1 September 2019.

Smith, Zadie. "Zadie Smith's rules for writers." *The Guardian*, 22 February 2010.

South African Reserve Bank. Presentation of the *Monetary Policy Review*. April 2020, Pretoria.

Southern African Legal Information Institute. "Standard Bank of South Africa Ltd v Dlamini (2877/2011) [2012] ZAKZDHC 64; 2013 (1) SA 219 (KZD) (23 October 2012)."

Strunk, Jr., William and E.B. White. *The Elements of Style.* Fourth edition. New York: Pearson, 2000.

Swift, Marvin H. "Clear writing means clear thinking means ..." *Harvard Business Review,* no. 73111 (January–February 1973): 58–62.

Temple, Emily. "Chimamanda Ngozi Adichie on how to write and how to read." *Literary Hub,* 15 September 2017.

Truss, Lynne. *Eats, Shoots & Leaves: The Zero Tolerance Approach to Punctuation.* London: Profile Books, 2003.

Victor, Daniel. "Oxford comma dispute is settled as Maine drivers get $5 million." *New York Times,* 9 February 2018.

Vonnegut, Kurt. "8 rules for writers." Quoted on the website of the Gotham Writers Workshop. Available at: https://www.writingclasses.com/toolbox/tips-masters/kurt-vonnegut-8-basics-of-creative-writing.

Wainaina, Binyavanga. "How to write about Africa." *Granta* 92, 2 May 2019.

Wolf, Martin. "The grasshoppers and the ants." *Financial Times,* 25 May 2010.

Yousafzai, Malala. "Malala Yousafzai: 'Our books and our pens are the most powerful weapons.'" *The Guardian,* 12 July 2013.

Zinsser, William. *On Writing Well.* Fifth edition. New York: HarperPerennial, 1994.

Zollner, Eckard. "What 4IR means in the context of South Africa." ICT Opinion South Africa. Bizcommunity, 20 August 2019.

ABOUT THE AUTHORS

DONALD POWERS is a senior editor and head of training and development at Clarity Global. He has two decades of experience as a writer, editor, lecturer and tutor in South Africa and Europe. He holds a PhD in English literature from the University of Cape Town.

GREG ROSENBERG has more than three decades of experience as a journalist, writer and editor. He is the co-founder of Clarity Global Strategic Communications in South Africa and the United States, and serves as a global advisor on public financial management communications.

Printed in the United States
by Baker & Taylor Publisher Services